# I BELIEVE
# IN IMMORTALITY

# I BELIEVE
# IN IMMORTALITY

*John Sutherland Bonnell*

**ABINGDON PRESS**

*New York* • *Nashville*

I BELIEVE IN IMMORTALITY

*Copyright © MCMLIX by Abingdon Press*

All rights in this book are reserved.
No part of the book may be used or reproduced in
any manner whatsoever without written permission of
the publishers except brief quotations embodied in
critical articles or reviews. For information address
Abingdon Press, Nashville 2, Tennessee.

*Library of Congress Catalog Card Number: 59-5206*

SET UP, PRINTED, AND BOUND BY THE
PARTHENON PRESS, AT NASHVILLE,
TENNESSEE, UNITED STATES OF AMERICA

*In Memoriam*

GEORGE CARRUTHERS,

M.D., C.M., F.R.C.S.

# CONTENTS

| ONE | IMMORTALITY | 9 |
| TWO | THE CERTITUDE OF ETERNAL LIFE | 23 |
| THREE | SKEPTICISM AND FAITH | 36 |
| FOUR | BODY AND SOUL | 53 |
| FIVE | THE POWER OF THE RESURRECTION | 73 |
| SIX | A PERSONAL CONFESSION OF FAITH | 88 |
| | NOTES | 95 |

# CHAPTER ONE

# IMMORTALITY

EVERY THOUGHTFUL PERSON HAS ASKED HIMSELF
this question: Does the life of man continue beyond the
grave? Try as we may to put the question out of our
thoughts, it will soon return. Death comes to all mankind.
It comes to the aged as they walk on faltering feet. Its
summons is heard by those who have scarcely reached
midway in life's journey, and often it hushes the laughter
of little children.

### The universality of death

This problem which teases and tortures the minds of
people today was never far from the thoughts of those of
ancient times. We see Cicero journeying to the Necropolis,
the City of the Dead, lighting a taper at the tomb of his
daughter, Tullia, and uttering the heartbroken cry: "Is
this the quenching of thy life, O my daughter?"

But love for those who are bound up in life's bundle
with us is not confined to the learned or the great. In
the homes of the humble and the poor, as well as in the
palaces of the wealthy, a cry of desolation is heard.

J. R. Green in *A Short History of the English People*
reveals that the question of immortality challenged the
thinking of our ancestors centuries ago. When Eadwine,
king of Northumbria and overlord of the whole of England, took for his wife the sister of the king of Kent, he

exposed himself to Christianity. With the queen came Paulinus, one of Augustine's followers, whose tall stooping form, slender aquiline nose, and black hair falling around a thin, worn face were long remembered in the north. The wise men of Northumbria gathered to discuss and weigh the reasons for and against the new faith to which Paulinus and the queen had speedily converted Eadwine. Christianity's appeal to the English people lay in the light it cast on the darkness that surrounded man's life and on the mystery of his origin and destiny.

During a discussion of the new religion an aged Ealdorman arose and said:

So seems the life of man, O king, . . . as a sparrow's flight through the hall when you are sitting at meat in winter-tide, with the warm fire lighted on the hearth, but the icy rainstorm without. The sparrow flies in at one door and tarries for a moment in the light and heat of the hearth-fire, and then flying forth from the other vanishes into the wintry darkness whence it came. So tarries for a moment the life of man in our sight, but what is before it, what after it, we know not. If this new teaching tells us aught certainly of these, let us follow it.

This is exactly what Christianity claims to do.

Death is the one tragic fact that no one can escape or deny. Job, centuries ago, pictured death in these words:

As the waters fail from the sea, and the flood decayeth and drieth up: So man lieth down, and riseth not: till the heavens be no more, they shall not awake, nor be raised out of their sleep.

But Job, like multitudes of his fellow men, rebelled at

10

this conclusion. He longed passionately for some evidence that man would live again.

## The universality of the belief

The first reason I would suggest for believing in immortality is *the universality of the belief*. All over the world people believe in it. Emerson wrote:

Here is this wonderful thought: Wherever man ripens, this audacious belief presently appears. . . . As soon as thought is exercised, this belief is inevitable. . . . Whence came it? Who put it into the mind of man?

Many books have been written on primitive concepts of immortality. We are especially indebted to Sir James G. Frazer for his Gifford Lectures delivered at St. Andrews University, Scotland. Here we find a full scientific record of the belief in a future life as it has been found among less civilized peoples of the world. He deals with the development of religion, including the idea of immortality, among the natives of British, Dutch, and French Guinea, among the Fiji Islanders, and even among the aborigines of Central Australia, who represent probably the lowest form of savage life of which we have scientific record. With almost no exception these people believed in some form of life after death. In this they were at one with the ancient civilizations of Greece, Egypt, and Rome and the peoples of Mesopotamia.

If only the more ignorant peoples of the world believed in a future life, we might wonder if they were not simply carrying into their waking hours the images and dreams of sleep. But the ablest and most independent thinkers have also grappled with the idea. Cicero said:

11

There is in the minds of men, I know not how, a certain presage, as it were, of a future existence; and this takes deepest root in the greatest geniuses and most exalted souls.

In this intuitive feeling for immortality, the deepest thinkers are at one with the humblest races of mankind.

Of course there are people who protest against such beliefs. H. L. Mencken scorned the thought of survival after death. He wrote:

What the meaning of human life may be I don't know. I am inclined to suspect that it has none. All I know about it is that to me at least it is very amusing while it lasts. . . . When I die, I shall be content to vanish into nothingness. No show, however good, could conceivably be good forever.

Prior to this he wrote: "I do not believe in immortality and have no desire for it. The belief in it issues from the puerile egos of inferior men."

Who are these "inferior" men to whom Mencken refers? They include scientific thinkers from Aristotle to Robert A. Millikan; philosophers from Plato and Socrates to Bergson; poets and dramatists such as Shakespeare, Milton, and Browning; unselfish souls such as Francis of Assisi, Livingstone, and Sir Wilfred Grenfell.

There have been in the past, as there are today, people who did not believe in immortality. But they were the exception. So Mencken refers to some of the finest minds of the race when he speaks of the "puerile egos of inferior men." Let James Martineau answer him:

Who are those who are "mistaken"? Not the mean and grovelling souls who have never reached to so great a thought. . . . No, the deceived are the great and holy whom all men

12

revere, the men who have lived for something better than their happiness and spent themselves on the altar of human good.

The fact that mankind in every age has believed in immortality is by no means a final proof that this concept is true. Yet it carries weight with thoughtful people.

## The nature of man

A second reason for believing in immortality is *the nature of man*. Man is gifted with what someone has described as a "vast overprovision." His mind is too great for the limitations of this world. He cannot fulfill himself in the brief space of time between the cradle and the grave. In so limited an existence his life is cramped, fragmented, incomplete.

Man is seldom satisfied. Unceasingly he aspires to what lies beyond his reach and is never able to accomplish fully the tasks he sets himself. This constant projection of man's mind and spirit is due to his kinship with God. God and man are spiritually alike. Man's mind is a small model of his creator's, and the universe is a mirror in which he sees the reflection of his own face.

If this were not true, there could be no science, for man would be unable to plot out the laws of the universe. So also there could be no revelation since man would possess no awareness of God and would therefore be unable to receive the truths which the Deity desires to impart.

Victor Hugo impressively emphasizes man's overendowment when, on his seventieth birthday, he writes:

Winter is on my head, and eternal spring is in my heart. The nearer I approach the end, the plainer I hear around me the immortal symphonies of the worlds which invite me. . . . For half a century I have been writing my thoughts in prose, verse, history, philosophy, drama, romance, tradition, satire, ode, song—I have tried all. But I feel that I have not said the thousandth part of what is in me.

Such testimony is ever on the lips of great men. All of us realize at times how small a part of our plans and aspirations will ever reach fruition in a lifetime. Nothing is plainer than that human life at its noblest and best falls far short of what our endowments might attain. The higher a man rises in the scale of life, the more earnestly he protests when his life's purposes are broken and his life's work is interrupted. He is pained to see his dreams unfulfilled. He knows that he has not contributed to the world more than a fraction of what is in him. Hidden powers and an undying spirit cry out for larger opportunity of expression. He is ever dissatisfied. His thirst for knowledge is never satisfied. God did not build our minds to fit them merely into the brief and fleeting life of earth, for we are constantly thinking "thoughts that wander through eternity." Goethe, the German philosopher and poet, was eighty-three when death called him. He answered with the cry on his lips: "Light! Light! More light!"

This sense of incompleteness is strongest in those who have the most to give to the world. So Corot at seventy-seven said: "If the Lord lets me live two years longer, I think I can paint something beautiful." Von Humboldt, the scientist, aspired far beyond this. When almost a century old he exclaimed, "Oh, for another hundred years!" Doubtless this "overprovision" was in Emerson's mind when he wrote, "God does not build magnificently for mice."

Equally impressive are the last words of men who were confident that eternal life awaited them beyond death. One such was Thomas Chalmers, Scotland's greatest preacher, who, on a quiet Sunday night, spoke words of cheery farewell to his family as he retired. His last utterance was far more prophetic than he or his could possibly know. He said, "I expect to give worship in the morning." His worship was given amid those eternal realities that God has prepared for those who love him.

So also passed the mighty reformer John Knox. His friend Richard Bannatyne sat beside his deathbed and read to his master words of scripture that Knox himself had often quoted: "This is life eternal, that they might know thee the only true God, and Jesus Christ, whom thou hast sent." The aged reformer hearing these words roused himself and with his dying breath said, "That is where I first cast my anchor."

The brevity of our lives here on earth becomes increasingly clear to us as we ourselves approach their close. We see this illustrated on every hand. The sculptor laboring at his masterpiece is bidden by death to lay down the chisel and the mallet. The statesman proclaims his vision of a world united in peace; and just as the words are spoken, death seals his lips. The preacher, growing in insight and power, plans his greatest sermon; but as he prepares the outline, the pen drops from his lifeless fingers.

A sense of imperfection and incompleteness clings to all things, for man is made in the image of his creator and demands something more than the world of space and time to fulfill his dreams. He requires eternity.

The hope of immortality which burns always in the heart of man originated in the distant past. It was kindled before Abraham had left his home in Ur of the Chaldees. It existed before the mighty pyramids reared their heads above the sandy wastes of Egypt. It had its beginning the moment man was able to reason.

As he rises in the scale of being, man's powers mount far beyond the limitations of the physical universe. The longer he lives and the more he progresses spiritually, the greater is the urge of his soul toward a perfection that it can achieve only in eternity. Man accomplishes in this world no more than the merest fragment of what he aspires to do. Death summons him when his work has scarcely begun. We have been built on too grand a scale to be satisfied with the limits of time. The one thing that saves us from futility and frustration is our hope that in an ampler theater that God has prepared, our highest powers will find satisfaction and fulfillment.

Man, like many another creature, is equipped for his environment. But his environment reaches far beyond his life on earth. Charles E. Jefferson refers to the adjustment of faculty to environment. He says:

Without sound vibrations there would be no ear. Without water there would be no fin. Without air there would be no wing. Whenever we find a faculty, we discover in the environment something to which that faculty responds. There is always a correspondence between the internal life and the external reality. This is true throughout the entire animal creation up to man. In man we find things which do not exist in animals below his rank. There is in him the thought of immortality, and the craving for it, and the expanding conviction of it. The question now arises, Is there any external reality to which this internal hope corresponds?

If we examine the structure of a pleasure craft on the Hudson River and an ocean liner like the Queen Mary, we see at once that one is intended for quiet inland waters while the other is built to sail the boundless main.

Likewise, if we compare man spiritually and mentally

16

with any other creature in nature, we find that he has capacities and endowments that enable him, as we believe, to sail "from out our bourne of Time and Place" into boundless seas.

The idea of immortality was in man's mind long before he began to formulate a philosophy to support it. Indeed the first valid philosophic arguments for human survival after death do not appear until the time of Plato. In the Athenian philosopher's *Phaedo* we find the first reasoned presentation of the case for the immortality and the indestructibility of the soul. But it must be admitted that though Plato's contention on this subject has been quoted for over two thousand years, it does not carry much weight with modern people. More impressive than the Greek philosopher's arguments is the passionate manner in which he presents them. John Baillie reminds us of the words of Jeremy Taylor in his funeral address for Sir George Dalston. Speaking of immortality, he said, "Men cast out every line, and turned every stone, and tried every argument: and sometimes proved it well, and when they did not, yet they believed strongly; and they were sure of the thing, when they were not sure of the argument."

Through the centuries men have continued to produce philosophic arguments, not because their case for the indestructibility of the soul was so convincing, but because they were so sure of the fact that they were driven to buttress it with philosophy.

These far-reaching beliefs and aspirations of man prophesy an eternity in which they will be realized.

### The purpose and reason of our universe
Again we find an intelligent basis for our belief in immortality in our *conviction that the universe unfolds a*

*purpose and a reason.* We cannot separate our faith in immortality from our view of the world. The materialist and the atheist can find no valid basis for such a faith.

Bertrand Russell writes:

No fire, no heroism, no integrity of thought and feeling can preserve an individual life beyond the grave; all the labors of the ages, all the devotion, all the inspiration, all the noonday brightness of human genius, are destined to extinction in the vast death of the solar system, and the whole temple of Man's achievement must inevitably be buried beneath the debris of a universe in ruins.

No one familiar with Russell's writings will be at all surprised at his conclusions. They are the certain result of his materialistic philosophy. At various times he has described the universe as irrational, blind to good and evil, mad, purposeless, senseless, monstrous. How could one holding such views by any stretch of the imagination believe in immortality?

But many of the best thinkers of our time have emphatically rejected Russell's bleak and despairing philosophy. Their repudiation is based on the belief that man's unique endowments can find no adequate explanation in the physical universe; that he is related to a spiritual order of being. So our world view is of supreme importance.

G. K. Chesterton in his whimsical fashion once wrote that if he were spending a holiday at Brighton, he would not ask his landlady the usual question, "What is the rent of your rooms?" Instead he would inquire, "What is your view of the universe?"

Our interpretation of the universe will shape our thinking on many important issues. Above all it will settle definitely whether or not we can believe in immortality. We believe in it because our concept of the universe and of its creator leads us to the faith that man made in the image of God is the final goal of the creative process.

Christians have frequently been charged with being naïve in their belief that man is of infinite worth to God. "Look at the universe around you," these critics say. "It is so large that it makes the earth look like an infinitesimal speck. Think of nature's waste when

> Of fifty seeds
> She often brings but one to bear."

But they are guilty of putting God on a level with man, and imply that he is interested only in immensity or material bulk and that he values only the things that can be measured, weighed, felt, and counted.

There is ample evidence in the world around us to support our belief that God created it to develop and perfect man, made in his image and capable of binding back the universe to its creator.

The star Betelgeuse, shining so brightly in the constellation of Orion, is larger than our whole solar system. Yet one human being is infinitely more important than Betelgeuse. Despite its huge size and the incalculable energy it generates, this star does not even know that it exists. The astronomer, who sets up his instruments on this ball of earth speeding through the sky, who weighs and measures Betelgeuse, analyzing its chemical elements and computing the physical laws that control it, dwarfs that distant star so far as higher values are concerned.

Michael Pupin, the famous physicist, enlarged on this thought:

The life of man is, as far as we know, the highest product of creation, and it is the most precious gift of heaven. . . . In the language of science it might be described as the climax of creative co-ordination.

The judgment of such thinkers is borne out by the fact that in man are gathered the noblest fruits of creation: beauty, goodness, truth, and love. These values have little meaning merely in the abstract. They have significance when they are embodied in human personality. There they take root and grow toward perfection. It is difficult to believe that the universe will destroy all traces of man who is the highest fulfillment of its creative activity. Not matter but man is supreme.

Tennyson expresses this faith in familiar verse:

> Tho' world on world in myriad myriads roll
> Round us, each with different powers,
> And other forms of life than ours,
> What know we greater than the soul?

Well may we ask: "Are man's highest spiritual qualities, into whose production so much of the creative energy of the universe has gone, doomed to disappear with the rest? Will this achievement go for nothing? Is it only a bubble that bursts or a vision that fades? Are we to regard the Creator's work as meaningless as that of a child who builds a house of blocks just for the pleasure of knocking it down again?"

Such a conclusion would rob us of the incentive to strive toward perfection, since it affirms that the highest is at the mercy of the lowest, and that our spirits are doomed by blind, material forces. Life itself and the testimony of men who are the intellectual and spiritual leaders of mankind deny such depressing conclusions.

In man we see a sublime faculty reaching out beyond

the things of sense to higher and vaster realms. Are we then to believe with the pessimist that there is no external Reality calling forth these hidden powers in man? Are we to believe that these hopes have been encouraged in the human soul only to be crushed and baffled? In that case the universe contradicts itself, and chaos is king.

John Stuart Mill stood with those who reject so desolating a conclusion. He believed it is not at all probable that God "would ordain the annihilation of His noblest and richest work, after the greater part of the few years of life had been spent in the acquisition of faculties which time has not allowed him to turn to fruit."

When Raphael died at the untimely age of thirty-seven, his last work, "The Transfiguration," was carried in the funeral procession to the Pantheon in Rome. The poet Rogers pictures the scene:

> And when all beheld
> Him where he lay, how changed from yesterday—
> Him in that hour cut off, and at his head
> His last great work; when entering in they looked
> Now on the dead, then on that masterpiece—
> Now on his face lifeless and colorless,
> Then on those forms divine that lived and breathed,
> And would live on for ages—all were moved,
> And sighs burst forth and loudest lamentations.

Has this masterpiece, which tens of thousands view with wonderment in the Vatican art gallery each year, outlived the spirit and personality of the man who created it? Have the fading outlines of Leonardo da Vinci's great painting "The Last Supper," still visible on the walls of the convent church of Santa Maria delle Grazie at Milan, outlasted the artist, or "The Last Judgment" in the Sistine

Chapel proved more enduring than Michelangelo who painted it?

Is the universe so organized that in the case of Raphael all these gifts and powers were suddenly wiped out by a fever germ? Man's mind refuses to accept such a conclusion. He cannot bear to think that the noblest souls who have walked our earth were at the mercy of physical events. He rejects the idea that the goodness that burned with so pure a flame in David Livingstone was extinguished by malaria, or in Phillips Brooks by diphtheria, or in Abraham Lincoln by an assassin's bullet.

We have every right to believe that all spiritual gains we make during our earthly life will be conserved in the life after death. The urge to perfection that lives in our hearts was not given us by accident. In the ampler theater of eternity we will have opportunity to develop our latent powers.

Paul, thinking of the life everlasting, wrote: "Now we see through a glass, darkly; but then face to face." In another letter he seemed to have the same thought in mind as he wrote: "But we all, with open face beholding as in a glass the glory of the Lord, are changed into the same image from glory to glory."

Henry Drummond inspires us with his rendering of the words "We are changed into the same image from glory to glory." He makes them read, "We are changed into the same image from character to character." So the good work which God has commenced in us during our earthly pilgrimage will be carried on to completion when the seen and the temporal are exchanged for the unseen and the eternal.

# CHAPTER TWO

# THE CERTITUDE
# OF ETERNAL LIFE

A LITTLE TIME AGO I RECEIVED FROM A SENIOR STUDENT of an American university a letter that said:

I am greatly troubled by a fact that has just come to my attention. I am unable to find a single argument for immortality in the whole of the New Testament. Actually Plato reasons on this subject in *Phaedo* more convincingly than Jesus ever did. How do you explain this?

It is quite true that Jesus never argued about immortality. As a philosophic idea it held very little interest for him. His concern was eternal life, which goes far beyond immortality.

Let us examine the word "immortality." Webster defines it as "exemption from death or annihilation; unending existence; everlastingness." Emmanuel Kant is more specific. He says that "immortality is the infinitely prolonged existence and personality of one and the same rational being."

Most of the definitions of immortality are passive, negative, and barren. We still speak of the "Christian doctrine of immortality." But these words do not mean the same thing that Jesus meant by eternal life. The concept of immortality does not necessarily carry the idea of progress and development. This type of immortality did not interest Jesus at all and had no place in his teaching. He never used the word "immortality." We find it only five times in the New Testament and not at all in the Gospels. The life of the world to come, as Jesus pictured it, is no such empty and meaningless concept as mere "unending existence." The criticism that the Christian doctrine of the future life presents a monotonous, futile existence is irrelevant.

## The attitude of agnostics

Take as an example the attitude of the famous lawyer and agnostic Clarence Darrow. Some years ago he toured the nation, debating with prominent clergymen and laymen on Christian beliefs. The idea that a human being after death enters upon an immortal life seemed to him especially absurd. As was his habit, Darrow offered his own definition of immortality and then vigorously attacked the straw man he had set up. He thought he was destroying belief in every form of immortality when he said: "No life is of much value, and every death is but a little loss. . . . The most satisfactory part of life is the time spent in sleep, when one is utterly oblivious to existence." He was speaking of life as he saw it, for he had found it to be largely disillusioning. If immortality meant an indefinite continuation of life as he had known it, he wanted none of it.

Schopenhauer, the German philosopher and pessimist, was even more bitter. He wrote: "To desire immortality is to desire the eternal perpetuation of a great mistake." Man's life he regarded as a supreme tragedy. We should do nothing to perpetuate the race, and the best we can look for is utter oblivion in death. Strangely enough, this grim, sour, bitter old man, when he had become famous and

24

had gained a little more of this world's goods, mellowed a great deal. He eventually was noted for his graciousness and hospitality. His home became a shrine visited by people from all over Germany, and he loved the homage of his adoring followers. How far this change in his environment and outlook altered his pessimistic philosophy is not recorded.

George Bernard Shaw once wrote a typically Shavian letter to a newspaper in London, declaiming against belief in immortality. He said he could scarcely imagine any greater calamity than that this "thing" called Shaw should go on forever "pouring forth thousands of plays and millions of newspaper articles." And many people would agree with him. It would indeed be an ordeal to have to spend an eternity listening to Shaw protest that his plays are better than Shakespeare's. But what does all this have to do with the Christian doctrine of eternal life?

The mood of Darrow, Schopenhauer, Shaw, and other writers who recoiled from the thought of life after death has been caught by Swinburne:

> From too much love of living,
>   From hope and fear set free,
> We thank with brief thanksgiving
>   Whatever gods may be
> That no life lives forever;
> That dead men rise up never;
> That even the weariest river
>   Winds somewhere safe to sea.

Here again we see a mood of boredom and defeat. What exactly is the idea that these writers are attacking? It is life *as they have experienced it* going on forever. Life for each of them has been a burden and a bore. They shared the concept of Buddha, who taught that existence is the greatest of evils.

Other critics of the idea of life after death say that such a belief is merely wishful thinking. Julian Huxley wrote:

I do not believe in immortality. A great danger of all religion is that it should embody wish-fulfillments, and the idea of immortality would appear to be merely the rationalization of wish-fulfillment.

We wonder if Huxley realized that he was wielding a two-edged sword, and one of the cutting edges was turned toward himself. This business of accusing people of "wishful thinking" works both ways. It may well be that the skeptical person who fights the idea of immortality on this basis is merely revealing his desire that his own futile and weary existence may be ended finally in death.

Informed Christian people agree fully with at least one part of the skeptic's argument. The life of a man who is bitter, cynical, and bored needs to come to an end. Indeed, if his life had to go on forever, it might well be one aspect of hell.

If someone asks us, "Do you wish to live forever?" our answer will be affected by what is meant by "forever," and also by the nature and quality of the life referred to. There are circumstances in which a Christian might well answer "no" to this question. What we are led to expect in such a future life might well determine our answer.

## The concept of eternal life

We have no record that Jesus ever discussed immortality as a philosophic idea. But he did emphasize the importance of believing in eternal life. He said, "I give unto them eternal life; and they shall never perish, neither shall any man pluck them out of my hand."

Jesus lays the supreme emphasis where it should be laid—on the quality of life after death and not merely on how long it will last.

On another occasion he said, "I am come that they might have life, and that they might have it more abundantly." It was this "more abundant" life that he promised his followers—a life beginning here and now and yet so rich and so meaningful in quality that death is powerless to bring it to an end. Eternal life according to Jesus is a full, deep, satisfying fellowship with God over which death has no power. Eternal life then is not so much a future reward as a present possession.

All men hunger for a true, deep, satisfying life. They shrink from the thought of emptiness and boredom, but yearn to live in deed and truth. Tennyson sings:

> 'Tis life, whereof our nerves are scant,
> Oh life, not death, for which we pant;
> More life, and fuller, that I want.

It was this "more life and fuller" which Jesus commended and which he unceasingly lived.

## Wistful agnosticism

Even an agnostic like Robert Ingersoll, who never entertained for himself the hope of life after death, longed for something akin to everlasting blessedness for those dear to him. In an eloquent tribute to the memory of his well-loved brother, he reported that mistaking the approach of death for the return of health, his brother had said, "I am better now." Ingersoll added, "May these dear words be true of all the countless dead."

In the same deeply moving address he went on to say:

Life is a narrow vale between the cold and barren peaks of two eternities. We strive in vain to look beyond the heights. We cry aloud—and the only answer is the echo of our wailing cry. From the voiceless lips of the unreplying dead there comes no word. *But in the night of Death Hope sees a star and listening Love can hear the rustle of a wing.* [Italics mine]

While this beautiful and poetic expression of hope falls far short of Christian conviction, nevertheless it reveals that even the skeptically minded sense on occasion the reality of the unseen and the eternal. We may, for a time, disregard the whispering voices that speak of spiritual things, but eventually they make themselves heard.

Centuries ago Augustine expressed the longing of the human soul for a fellowship and a peace that only God can give: "Thou hast made us to incline to thee, and our hearts are restless and tormented until in thee they find their peace."

The reality of this inner peace Jesus constantly proclaimed. He not only declared it; he experienced it. He assured his disciples that death could not end their fellowship with God. He spoke in words that for simplicity and quiet power surpass anything that has ever been spoken or written. He told his followers that death would simply usher them into his presence. On the night of the betrayal, with the shadow of the Cross looming over the little company, the Master said:

In my Father's house are many rooms; if it were not so, would I have told you that I go to prepare a place for you? And when I go and prepare a place for you, I will come again and will take you to myself, that where I am you may be also.

The New Testament does not claim that Jesus Christ

28

originated the hope of immortality. But it does declare that he vastly enriched it. He gave the concept new and deeper meaning. Paul expressed the thought of all the followers of the Master when he wrote: "Jesus Christ, who hath abolished death, and hath brought life and immortality to light through the gospel."

Our Lord portrayed eternal life as possessing a quality so full of meaning, so radiant, so filled with spiritual growth and joy and peace that it is worth going on with through all eternity. And this hope Jesus based squarely on *the character of God*.

## Plato's idea of immortality

This is a distinctively Hebrew and Christian idea. Plato in his *Phaedo* bases his argument for immortality on such considerations as the uniqueness of man, and finds in his moral endowments and constitution the demand for immortality. He stresses the fact that man is a moral being. He is subject to the constraint of moral law. The roots of man's life reach out into the unseen and the eternal. He is impelled by duty. Therefore his true being belongs more to the laws and life of eternity than to time.

Christian thinkers are in full agreement with this aspect of Plato's argument about man. Man requires the life of the world to come so that he may fulfill the moral and spiritual endowments given to him. The higher he rises in the spiritual scale, the more he becomes aware of his own incompleteness. Paul writes: "Not that I have already obtained this or am already perfect; but I press on. . . ."

Man needs time, infinite time, to reach his goal. At this point we may say with Browning:

> Was it not great? did not he throw on God,
> (He loves the burthen) —

29

God's task to make the heavenly period
Perfect the earthen?

But the Bible, and especially the New Testament, goes
far beyond man's powers or endowments for evidence on
which to base belief in immortality. Its proof is in the
character of God. The scriptures constantly emphasize
that God wills to enter into intimate, personal relationship with each man and woman. The New Testament goes
so far as to describe one Old Testament character as "the
friend of God." It thus implies that God himself found
something in Abraham that provided the basis of an intimate fellowship.

## Eternal life as friendship with God

This friendship with God is the pledge, the promise,
and the unfailing assurance of eternal life. This is the
highest point of spirituality reached in the Old Testament,
and it is brought to full fruition in the New. We see it
emerging again in Job. Turning away from the depressing
spectacle of death's seeming victory, he utters the tri-
umphal cry, "I know that my redeemer liveth." Knowing
that mortality and decay will do their worst, he is yet able
to say, "I shall see God."

We find this hope soaring again in the sixteenth psalm.
Says the psalmist:

> For thou dost not give me up to Sheol,
> or let thy godly one see the Pit.
> Thou dost show me the path of life.

He believes that his final destiny is to be not death but
life—life in the presence of the God who has been the
companion and the guide of his pilgrimage.

Our Lord begins where the prophets and seers of the Old Testament leave off. He carries forward to lofty heights the hope of eternal life. The scribes and Pharisees and doctors of the law tried to snare Jesus with deceptive questions about the life of the world to come. But the Master threw them into confusion and destroyed the people's confidence in them by his overwhelming response.

Ye do err, not knowing the scriptures, nor the power of God. . . . Have ye not read that which was spoken unto you by God, saying, I am the God of Abraham, and the God of Isaac, and the God of Jacob? God is not the God of the dead, but of the living.

In these words Jesus not only plainly implied that God is the God of individual men and women with whom he maintains a personal relationship, but he also inferred that this bond of fellowship is not broken by death. Luke adds these words of Jesus: *"For all live unto him."* An unbroken friendship with their heavenly Friend is the reward of those who love and trust him. But *present* friendship with God is the pledge of this relationship in eternity. As Jesus said, "No man is able to pluck [you] out of my hand." And Paul adds:

I am persuaded, that neither death, nor life, nor angels, nor principalities, nor powers, nor things present, nor things to come, nor height, nor depth, nor any other creature, shall be able to separate us from the love of God, which is in Christ Jesus our Lord.

God's character is our unfailing guarantee that he will never abandon those who have been called into fellowship with him. The strength of this pledge of eternal life lies in

31

the fact that the believer experiences its meaning and quality in his life here on earth, and thus comes to know that through this fellowship with God an unbreakable bond has been forged that even death cannot sever.

P. T. Forsyth says, "To live for Eternity is much, but to live Eternity is more." This statement conveys a deep understanding of the meaning of eternal life as the New Testament depicts it. The Christian is in eternity every moment of his earthly life. Our citizenship in celestial abodes is not a hope to which we look forward. It is no outward validation; it is within us. The question we ought to ask ourselves frequently is this: Am I living as an immortal being now rather than as one who is endeavoring to qualify for immortality? Let us ever remember that the immortality of the New Testament is a gift bestowed on us by God's free grace and is not something for which we work or a human right on which we presume. Entirely too often in Christian circles the whole issue of immortality descends to the level of a theoretical discussion rather than a practical issue that vitally concerns day-by-day living. Our expectation of eternal life raises our common tasks and struggles above the trivial to the sublime. It enhances the soul's morale and imparts to it a sense of worth.

Schleiermacher writes: "For religion, immortality means being one with the Infinite in the midst of finitude. It means to be eternal at every moment." These words are in full agreement with New Testament teaching. The more our thoughts are turned to the life everlasting and the greater our endeavor to live by its laws, the more do we inhabit another and a higher world.

There are those who suggest that if this life were the end of man's existence, it would make all his relationships still more precious. It would seem, however, that Tennyson is nearer the truth when he says that unless we are sure of love's immortality, a blight would lay hold on it and it would be "Half dead to know that it could die." It would be difficult for love, either to God or man, to survive such a depressing thought.

## The firm assurance of faith

During World War I in the twenty-first Casualty Clearing Station at Merville, France, a critically wounded soldier lay on a cot near mine. I heard the chaplain say to him, "The medical officer tells me that you cannot recover. I am sure that you will want to know the truth. But don't be afraid, lad, for God is with you."

The young soldier gazed steadily into the chaplain's eyes and said, "I'm not afraid, Padre. It's my last trip 'over the top' but I'm not going out alone." What did he mean?

Many a night this young soldier had gone "over the top" into the shell-swept area of no man's land with death lurking on every side. But always he had been able to master his fears, for he became aware of Another beside him whose presence kept him steadfast. Now when the sands of life were running out, he knew that the Friend who had never failed him would be with him on the last and greatest adventure of all. *He was not going out alone.* "My Father, which gave them me," said Jesus, "is greater than all; and no man is able to pluck them out of my Father's hand."

## The fatherhood of God

We find ourselves groping for an illustration to make clear the truth of these words. There comes to me across the years the memory of an experience when I was fifteen years old. It was always a great event when I was able to spend a week end with my father at the mental hospital where for forty-six years he was supervisor. One Friday night I set out across the fields to visit him. It was a walk of three miles. The moon was shining brightly as I strode on. Scarcely had I gone a mile when the skies clouded, and the moon disappeared. Darkness clothed the countryside. A wooded area towered before me. Time and again I found myself off the pathway, and the only way I could find it again was by kneeling down and feeling for it with my hands. I remembered with satisfaction that at the end of what we called the "green road" there would be a light burning at the white gate that led into the grounds of the hospital.

As I looked far ahead, trying to pierce the darkness, I saw to my dismay that the light was not burning. As I listened intently, I could hear the snap of twigs in the woods, and with the vivid imagination of boyhood pictured some denizen of the night on the prowl. I could feel my heart pounding as I broke into a run. But the more I hurried, the more frightened I became. Then directly ahead I heard another sound. Someone was walking toward me. Suddenly out of the darkness came a familiar voice saying, "Is that you, son?" It was my father's voice! Then he added, "I just discovered that the light was out at the gate so I came to meet you." In that moment a miracle happened. The night was no longer dark, for I was now walking with my father.

Out of the darkness and horror of Calvary came the voice of the crucified saying, "Father, into thy hands I commend my spirit." And the dark was no longer dark, for he was with his Father. He had come from God, and

34

he went to God. So also those who walk with God in this earthly pilgrimage know from blessed experience that he will not abandon his children who trust in him. In the night of death his presence will be "better than a light and safer than a known way."

# CHAPTER THREE

# SKEPTICISM AND FAITH

MANKIND IN GENERAL HAS WIDELY ACCEPTED FAITH in some form of immortality. Nevertheless there has always been a large segment of the race that has rejected the concept. In this group at times have been well-known men and women. It is significant, however, that even those who cannot believe in the victory of life over death shrink from the thought of ultimate annihilation.

Thomas Huxley, the agnostic, doubted. Yet at the age of sixty we find him writing:

> It is a curious thing that I find my dislike of the thought of extinction increasing as I get older. It flashes across me at all times with a sort of horror that in 1900 I shall probably know no more than I did in 1800. I had rather be in hell.

Thomas Hardy, the British novelist and poet, whose dust was laid to rest in Westminster Abbey, accepted the creed of fatalism. But his allegiance to this desolate creed often wavered. He longed for true faith. A few years before his death, at the age of eighty-eight, he was visited in his beloved Wessex by a nearby church choir that sought to honor him. He asked the leader of the choir, "Will you people please sing for me a hymn that has been in my mind of late?" The hymn that Thomas Hardy asked for was this:

Sun of my soul, Thou Saviour dear,
It is not night if Thou be near.

It may well be that the famous author, when he felt the night of death closing around him, laid hold upon these words in the secret hope that there might yet be light at eventide.

Those who doubt the existence of the immortal life have oftentimes protested their own conclusions while the wisest and best men of our race have cherished this hope. Likewise, the man who believes with assurance in the immortality of the soul is more likely to dedicate himself to life's highest purposes and the well-being of his fellow men. Such a faith is a spur to nobler living. Even Renan, the skeptic, was impressed by this fact. He wrote that "The day in which the belief in an afterlife shall vanish from the earth will witness a terrific moral and spiritual decadence." How could it be otherwise? Such a conclusion would mean that matter is triumphant over spirit and that man's soul is at the mercy of "a few particles of disordered dust." It would mean that the noblest man who ever lived would be less enduring than a clod of common clay.

## Disillusionment and cynicism

In the period following World War I a wave of disillusionment and cynicism swept across the United States. The faith of many faltered. Nowhere was skepticism more rampant than in the universities. Hundreds of young people surrendered to the mood of despair. One of the most brilliant graduates of an eastern university wrote me a letter fairly dripping with pessimism and a sense of futility. Its last paragraph read as follows: "I suppose that my impotency, my puerility, and my utter blankness in the face of the eternal enigma is one of the reasons for the fits of utter depression into which I fall at times."

It is not surprising that an epidemic of suicides swept across American campuses. A college teacher thoroughly familiar with the American scene said:

The reason for this was the fact that our universities succeeded in convincing a lot of young people that they are but "an accidental collocation of atoms," or "a cunningly devised machine," and so, when they met with disappointments and frustrations in life, they asked themselves, "Why shouldn't I dissolve the atoms or stop the mechanism?"

Edwin Arlington Robinson was doubtless thinking in this vein when he wrote:

> If after all that we have lived and thought,
> All comes to Nought,—
> If there be nothing after Now,
> And we be nothing anyhow,
> And we know that,—why live?

On the other hand, the person who girds himself with the faith that "life is ever lord of death" stands magnificently unscathed. He is not bitter. Life's experiences cannot hurt him. No matter how hard the battle goes, he knows that it is worthwhile, for in the long run it will produce indestructible gains. A striking illustration of this is seen in the experience of Sir Wilfred Grenfell of the Labrador. I talked with him in Florida a few months before his death and felt the warm glow of his faith. Never have I known a more radiant personality or one who faced the future with such serenity. In his autobiography he writes:

It has been my lot in life to stand by many deathbeds and

to be called in to dying men and women almost as a routine of my profession. Yet I am increasingly convinced that they never die at all. I am sure that there is no real death. . . . Eternal life is the complement of all my unsatisfied ideals. Experience teaches me that belief in it is a greater incentive to be useful and good than anything that I know.

Toward the close of an address that he gave to a group of people in the garden of a Miami home, he said, "It seems the most natural thing in the world to me to pass through the door of death into everlasting life." A still higher concept of life eternal, as we have already noted, is to know it as a present possession rather than a future hope.

## The spirit of secularism

One of the greatest enemies of religion in general, and belief in immortality in particular, is the spirit of *secularism*. Secularism is the organization of life without reference to God or spiritual reality. It utterly destroys those high religious convictions that put granite into the character of our forefathers. Today secularism is sweeping over civilization like the slow spread of a sea of lava. It proclaims that all man's improvements can be achieved by material means alone. Faith in God and immortality are regarded as obstacles to progress. Multitudes of people who would be at a loss to explain the philosophy of secularism are nevertheless under its sway. We no longer possess that assurance of divine guidance and blessing that was so powerful in the lives of the pioneers who laid firm and strong the foundations of America. It gave them courage and faith as they set forth to subdue the earth and to push ever forward the frontiers of the new world.

This ever-widening spirit of secularism is a greater

enemy of the Christian faith than an army of atheists. It is attacking us today in the field of education. We proclaim the right of every boy and girl in our nation to an education. That in itself is excellent, but what do we mean by an education? Walter Lippmann says: "We have established a system of education in which we insist that while everyone must be educated, yet there is nothing in particular that an educated man should know."

Has education no reference to character? Can it safely ignore such fundamentals as God, the moral law, and immortality? Should we not have some assurance as to how the student will use his new insights and knowledge?

## Education and spiritual principles

Lord Macaulay attacked bitterly the idea that education could afford to do away with moral and spiritual principles. He wrote:

As if history were not made up of the bad actions of extraordinary men . . . as if nine-tenths of the calamities which have befallen the human race had any other origin than the union of high intelligence with low desires.

"The union of high intelligence with low desires"— that is the peril of some types of education that leave no place for character building, moral discipline, or faith in God and immortality.

We must admit that American education, especially in technical fields, has, up to the present, led the world. The fact remains, however, that many colleges of our nation give religion an unfriendly reception. Or else they treat it as though it were a small, unimportant addendum to life. One of the largest universities on the eastern seaboard

40

offers as recommended reading in one of its courses, *The Absurdities of Christianity.*

Intelligence and education alone cannot provide an answer to our most stubborn problems. If every citizen in the nation earned and received a college diploma, our moral disabilities could still remain as obstacles barring us from our highest goals. There might well continue to be the perilous union of "high intelligence with low desires."

Dr. Thomas Arnold, headmaster of the famous boys' school at Rugby, England, defined his ideal of education as "the training of a Christian gentleman." Character building was thus a first consideration at Rugby. When we think of the character of a gentleman, we think of truthfulness, honor, fair play, public spiritedness, and nobleness. But these high qualities cannot stand alone, like a flower cut off from its roots. So Arnold speaks of a "Christian gentleman." He is aware of the need of a philosophy of life to support these ideals and of a faith to help them grow.

## Secularism and life's meaning

Secularism shows itself in another way. It robs life of any serious meaning or purpose. When a man becomes skeptical of God and immortality, he loses his greatest possible incentive to worthwhile living. Tens of thousands of men and women in our time are living shallow, fleeting lives that reveal no hint of an eternal destiny.

In the summer of 1931 the news was flashed across this nation that Ralph Barton, the gifted caricaturist, had committed suicide. I shall retell the story of his life as it was briefly recorded in more than one American publication.

Barton's undisputed talents won for him world acclaim.

Before he died, this gifted man wrote a letter. It is a momentous document, because it shows us the emptiness and folly of modern sophistication. He addressed it to the public. In it he recorded the story of his successes: his glamorous life, the honors and adulations lavished on him, his constant round of pleasures, while he gave little thought to the harm he did to other lives.

Then followed a paragraph worthy of a place in Dante's *Purgatorio:*

I have run from wife to wife, from house to house, and from country to country, in a ridiculous effort to escape from myself. In so doing I am very much afraid that I have brought a great deal of unhappiness to those who have loved me. . . . No one thing is responsible for this [suicide] and no one person except myself. . . . I did it because I am fed up with inventing devices for getting through twenty-four hours a day.

Ralph Barton drew many a caricature with his pencil, but the most remarkable portrait he ever painted was this one of himself.

If on the other hand we can succeed in organizing our lives around lofty ideals, we shall have found a faith to live by and a purpose to live for. We have only to look about us to see abundant examples of this truth. The man who organizes his life around Jesus' concept of eternal life widens his horizons and learns how to live *sub specie aeternitatis*—under the form or aspect of eternity. He is able to face all life's vicissitudes with serenity and courage.

## Skepticism and the fact of death

Oftentimes a momentous experience in life shakes a man out of his self-satisfied skepticism. When life tumbles in, he needs something more than "the firm foundations

of unyielding despair" or a head that is "bloody, but un-
bowed."

An author who was immensely popular with the masses
of the English people wrote a book some time since called
*God and My Neighbor*. In this book he attacked with vigor
the accepted Christian beliefs such as God, Christ, prayer,
and immortality. The author, Robert Blatchford, was not
very modest about the results he expected from his book.
He believed that he had succeeded in completely demolish-
ing Christianity. This is what he wrote:

> I claim to have proved everything I set out to prove so fully
> and decisively that no Christian, however great or able he may
> be, can answer my arguments or shake my case.

Blatchford surrounded himself with a wall of blatant
skepticism. Then a surprising thing happened. His wall
suddenly crumbled to dust. He was left exposed and
undefended. Slowly he began to feel his way back to the
faith that he had scorned and ridiculed.

What had caused this profound change in his outlook?
His wife died. They had journeyed so long together that
he hadn't realized the possibility of separation. With a
broken heart he went into the room where all that was
mortal of her lay. He looked again at the face he loved
so well. Coming out he said to a friend:

> It is she, and yet it is not she. Everything is changed. Some-
> thing that was there before is taken away. She is not the same.
> What can be gone if it be not the soul?

A few years later we find a gentler, kindlier, humbler
Robert Blatchford writing a new book. No longer does he

boast that he has destroyed faith in immortality. But he writes:

Death is not what some people imagine. It is only like going into another room. In that other room we shall find . . . the dear women and men and the sweet children we have loved and lost.

Death, with its devastating impact on man's life, has shattered many a smug and confident philosophy. It forces all of us to think. It is a great educator. All people, whether or not they have faith, possess one thing in common. They look on death as an intruder. It is an enemy that suddenly appears in the midst of life's feast, putting out its lights and gaiety.

Philosophers and poets have reminded us that we cannot avoid death, for it passes no one by. They have mused on its impenetrable mysteries. So Omar Khayyám sings:

Strange, is it not? that of the myriads who
Before us passed the door of Darkness through,
  Not one returns to tell us of the Road,
Which to discover we must travel too.

Death lays its hand upon those dear to us and leaves us baffled and wondering. In exceptional situations, as when someone is suffering greatly in a hopeless illness, death comes as an angel of mercy. But for the most part we think of it as the enemy of human happiness.

## The scientific spirit

Some Christian people have felt that the impact of the scientific spirit in the last half-century has weakened man's faith in immortality. During this period a revolution

44

occurred in man's processes of thought. A new way of looking at the universe came into being. Not a single area of life has been unaffected by its influence. This new viewpoint begins by examining the facts, then moves on to theories and general ideas. The older method of philosophy began with general ideas and used these ideas to interpret the facts. According to science we do not assume anything. We sit down before the facts and try to find the final meaning. Thus bit by bit we may discover the truth about life.

Timid souls feared that science would turn the world upside down. They were afraid it would destroy the foundation of man's life. We have used the new approach to examine one branch of science after another: physics and the make-up of matter, biology and the origin of life, physiology and the human body, psychology and the laws of the mind, astronomy and the heavenly bodies. Finally men began to apply the scientific method to religion. Scholars have turned its searchlight on the Bible. They examined its books one by one. They checked the authors, dates, and contents. Last of all they studied the life of Jesus and the claims Christian people have made on his behalf. They investigated thoroughly the historical reality of Jesus. Some Christians asked, "By what right do we apply the scientific method to the sacred text of the Bible?" But other and wiser Christians answered, "Why not? If Christianity and the Bible deal with abiding and eternal truth, what are we afraid of? What has truth to fear from the explorations of science?" When scholars in Britain were studying the books of the Bible, an organization known as the Bible Defense Association was formed. One member of it wrote Charles Haddon Spurgeon and asked him to join. He replied: "The title is an impertinence.

The Bible needs no defense. The Bible is a lion. Let it loose among the people. It will defend itself."

Christianity and the holy Scriptures have emerged stronger than ever. Their central postulates—the sovereignty of God, the moral law, the spiritual uniqueness and supremacy of Jesus as the Son of God and the revealer of God to man, as well as faith in eternal life stand as firm and enduring as they did before the scientific method had been discovered.

## Scientific neutrality

We must remember that the scientific method is an intellectual and analytical approach to reality. It is concerned with the "how" of the universe. Religion and philosophy, on the other hand, seek to answer the questions "Whence?" "Why?" and "Whither?" The areas of science and religion have now been defined sufficiently that there need not and should not be any conflict between these two sister forces engaged in the search for truth. Actually, science as science has no answer to the question, "Is there a life after death?" Science has no reason even to ask this question. The best that even scientists who believe in immortality can say is that science as science is completely neutral. Science, however, has produced no evidence that contradicts such a belief or that discredits it in any way. Indeed, many scientists, speaking as Christian men, profess faith in immortality. And science itself appears to give this widely-held belief its "vote to be so if it can."

There have been those among scientists who have publicly proclaimed their denial of belief in any form of immortality. In Britain in 1927, Arthur Keith, who was then president of the British Association for the Advancement of Science, declared that he could under no circumstances believe in immortality. His successor in the presidency of the same association, William Henry Bragg, the noted physicist and Nobel Prize winner, the following year publicly declared that he did believe in immortality. Each of these men stated his belief on personal, not scientific, grounds.

Unfortunately, however, some authors have been in the habit of speaking of this or that position as "adopted by science" on the question of religion, and specifically on immortality. Bertrand Russell comments on his philosophy of materialism: "Such is the world which science presents for our belief." We can, however, quote a score of able, living scientists who would not hesitate to say, "Science presents no such world view."

A professor of philosophy at Princeton University a few years ago wrote that the "findings of science" supported his view that we live in a universe without sense, or purpose, or reason. In the science department of the same university, at the same time, Albert Einstein was writing, "All but the crudest scientific work is based on a firm belief akin to religious feeling, in the rationality and comprehensibility of the world."

The fact remains that anything scientists say for or against religion, even though it be only their own personal viewpoint, takes on great importance. So large is the prestige of science at the present time that some people are unduly encouraged or distressed by the attitude of an individual scientist toward religious faith.

## Marie Curie

When Marie Curie's biography was published, there came to my desk a letter from a college student. He wrote:

47

I have been reading the biography of Madame Curie and greatly fear that it will have an adverse effect on Christian faith. Here was a noble woman, a scientist, who believed neither in God nor in immortality.

In reply I wrote:

Never fear what this book will do to faith. If it will have any influence on religion at all, it will show how bleak and lonely is even the noblest life consecrated to science when it lacks a sustaining faith, and is hemmed in by the confines of death and the grave. This is why so many people have found it a dreadfully depressing book.

Do you recall the day when Pierre Curie was killed in an accident in the streets of Paris? From that hour Marie Curie was a doomed woman. On the night of the funeral she went home and made this entry in her diary:

They filled the grave and put sheaves of flowers on it. Everything is over. Pierre is sleeping his last sleep beneath the earth. It is the end of everything, everything, everything.

But that was not the most tragic episode. Weeks later, when with her sister Bronya she was destroying the suit her husband wore on the day of the accident, she found bits of cloth bearing on them fragments of decay and death. Eagerly she seized these pieces of Pierre's clothing and kissed them again and again until her sister dragged them out of her hands and flung them into the fire. Why shouldn't she treasure them? She believed that this was all that was left of the one she loved—the poor, pitiful fragments of corruption and mortality and decay.

## *Faith triumphant*

As we turn from this depressing picture, let me illustrate what faith in God and immortality can do for a man. I have in my files a letter written by Kenneth Munro, one-time minister of the historic American Presbyterian Church of Montreal. All his friends rejoiced when he was called to that great church because we knew that it was the beginning of a splendid ministry. Our hopes were justified. He increased in power from month to month, becoming one of Canada's foremost preachers. Then suddenly and unexpectedly tragedy came. He was laid aside by illness, and the doctor said, "We are not going to withhold the truth from you. There is not the slightest hope of a cure."

All the dreams he had dreamed of his great church dissolved into black and impenetrable shadows. As the end was nearing, he wrote a letter, a copy of which I have in my files. It was addressed to his congregation:

You will have the right to say to me now, "You often told us to be calm and confident in the hour of death. Are you calm and confident now? You told us that we ought to believe in God. Have you that faith?"

I will give you the answer. What I want to say to you, and it may be the most effective sermon I have ever preached, is that God has given me a victory so wonderful and a peace so sure and deep that I don't know what it is unless it be "the peace that passeth all understanding." I want you to know that God gave me a happiness so wonderful that I found myself praising God over and over again for the strange experience which seemed such a frustration of all my hopes. Death lost every vestige of terror. Indeed, I could think of no better description of what happened to me than to put it into the words of the apostle, "He hath destroyed death."

I cannot tell you the effect it had upon my soul when I realized that the gospel is true and that it works. A sense of confidence and strength and peace suffused my whole being, and now for the first time in my life my soul seems to be garrisoned with a peace which is not disturbed by a single doubt.

Little wonder that when the funeral services for him began in that great church in Montreal, the organ pealed forth the stirring "Hallelujah Chorus," for a great servant of Christ was standing at attention in the presence of his king.

I have been writing about certain philosophies that carry with them glimpses of immortality. But we do well to remember that there are promptings of the heart as well as of the head that we ought not to disregard. Pascal has said, "The heart hath reasons that the reason doth not know."

## Love and immortality

We cannot doubt that love stands supreme among all the values known to man. Without it our lives would become as cold and barren as would our earth if it lost the warmth and light of the sun.

Now if the Christian hope of eternal life be but a delusion, then love is finally defeated, for immortality implies union with those we love. The noisiest skeptic, no matter how he may try to rationalize his own attitudes, rebels fiercely at the thought of death's power to disrupt and utterly destroy. Try as he will, he cannot get used to the thought of such an abrupt and final separation.

Tennyson faced this problem in the death of a friend. At the first painful impact it seemed that for him the end of the world had come. Yet he, with multitudes of others, found that it is impossible for love to believe that death ends all. Love springs back from that thought with a cry of pain. His dearest college friend, Arthur Hallam, had died; and Tennyson felt that his own heart had been laid away in the tomb. His poem *In Memoriam* is a noble tribute to his friend. In it Tennyson tells of all the doubts and fears that passed in a long procession through his mind. He reviews the questions that science and philosophy raise with respect to immortality. At times he had to battle to keep his faith. He could argue deeply with the skeptics, but it was always his heart that carried him through. He wrote:

> If e'er when faith had fall'n asleep,
>   I heard a voice "Believe no more;"
>   And heard an ever-breaking shore
> That tumbled in the Godless deep,
>
> A warmth within the breast would melt
>   The freezing reason's colder part,
>   And like a man in wrath the heart
> Stood up and answer'd, "I have felt."

Our greatest poets have united with many of the best minds of the race in the faith

> That Life is ever lord of Death,
>   And Love can never lose its own!

To Ralph Waldo Emerson we give the last word: Standing by the open grave of his little boy, he pondered this problem and afterward wrote:

> What is excellent
> As God lives, is permanent;

51

Hearts are dust, hearts' loves remain;
Hearts' love will meet thee again.

This is the faith that triumphs over skepticism. It enables us to face life's deepest tragedies in the sure and certain hope that no matter how dark and desolate the night may be, "joy cometh in the morning."

# CHAPTER FOUR

# BODY AND SOUL

ALFRED G. FISK IN A THOUGHT-PROVOKING CHAPTER ON
immortality writes:

> The only really important argument against belief in per-
> sonal immortality is that our personality, ego, self, soul (what-
> ever it is called) is in this life . . . indissolubly connected with
> the body, dependent on the body.

If this argument be valid, when the body is destroyed
and death takes place, the ego, self, or soul ceases to be.
In such an eventuality we may ask whether there can be
any separate "soul" or "self" that has a future life apart
from the body.

From the available evidence we have it would appear
that the body has a determinative influence on the mind
or soul. For instance, if a certain part of a man's brain be
injured, he may completely forget a language he has
known. A professor of classics suffered a head injury that
completely destroyed his knowledge of Greek. The mind
appears to be dependent not only on the brain, as the
episode of the Greek scholar seems to show, but it is also
affected by damage to parts of the sympathetic nervous
system. Again, is not the mind as well as the body affected
by a certain quantity of alcohol? If sufficient alcohol were
taken to destroy the body, would the lethal dose not also
destroy the mind or soul? In other instances the result

of an accident has been complete amnesia, or even mental illness. Yet taking all the evidence into account, we cannot be certain that the self or soul has been created by the body or has had a physical origin.

On the other hand, we have impressive evidence that the mind, soul, or self influences the body to a marked degree. A change of thought or an emotional disturbance can have a discernible effect on the body. The newer emphasis on psychosomatic medicine has emerged from the fact that the mind produces many ills in the body. The mind thus becomes an agent or promoting cause. Dr. J. A. Hadfield produces scientific evidence which "will encourage us in the belief that in the course of evolution the mind shows an ever-increasing tendency to free itself from physical control and, breaking loose from its bonds, to assert its independence and live a life undetermined except by the laws of its own nature." A century ago materialistic scientists rallied their forces around the slogan "The brain secretes thought as the liver secretes bile." But he would be a bold materialist who would dare to make that assertion today!

## The brain as an instrument of thought

John Fisk in his Ingersoll Lectures at Harvard University quoted the saying "No thought without a brain." Then he commented, "If you refer to the present life, most erudite professor, your remark is true, but hardly erudite or startling; if you refer to any condition of things subsequent to death, pray where did you obtain your knowledge?" He pointed out that man's awareness is far from being limited to the physical. We cannot doubt that there are immense regions of existence just as real as those we know, yet of them we have only a very inadequate knowledge.

If we are conscious only because of a certain shifting of molecules within the brain, then we shall inevitably lose consciousness when the molecules no longer vibrate. Granted this premise, the materialist would be correct in declaring that the relation of conscious intelligence to the brain is the same as the relation of music to the harp. When the strings of the harp are broken, the music will no longer be heard.

There does appear to be evidence that thought is always accompanied by activity in the molecules of the brain. But this is quite a different matter from saying that these physical vibrations produce or create thinking. We have ample justification for claiming that the brain is not the creator of thought but rather its instrument. It is a significant fact that man's personality is not altered though every cell of his body is made over during each interval of seven years. The unbroken continuity of memory is a proof of this. His "ego" or "self" always retains its identity and yet continues to be united with the body in some mysterious manner that science cannot explain. Sir Wilfred Grenfell expressed it in this way,

I am now living in my ninth body, but I have not changed through all these years. This body of mine is a medium that I have constantly used, discarding one body after another.

## Personality and the human body

Man is without doubt a dual being. On the physical side he is allied to the rest of creation. Certain organs of his body are similar to those of the higher animals. But these are not his distinguishing characteristic. That which sets

55

man apart from all the remainder of creation is his personality, or self, or soul.

R. Rennie Swan, in his presidential address to the Winnipeg Medical Society, put it like this:

Man is not simply made up of flesh. It is impossible to explain him in terms of flesh alone. I inhabit my body and use it, but my body is not "I." I look out through my eyes; I work with my hands; I speak with my lips, but neither eyes nor hands nor lips, nor all of them put together are "I." The real "I" is something within, invisible, intangible, imponderable, which directs, controls, and governs this physical frame. That thinking, feeling, willing something is the real "I." We know that the body cells are continuously changing, but the "I" remains. I possess a totally different body from that which I possessed as a boy. If my body were "I," I should be an entirely different "I" from what I was forty-five years ago. But I know I am not a different "I." I am conscious that the lad of four decades ago and the man of today are one and the same person.

Man is a combination of dust and divinity. The story of his creation in the second chapter of Genesis affirms this. "And the Lord God formed man of the dust of the ground, and breathed into his nostrils the breath of life; and man became a living soul."

Years ago while browsing through some old magazines, I came upon an article in a journal of archaeology. It told the story of some excavators who had broken into an underground tomb. For one fleeting moment they saw on a ledge of rock the body of a beautiful maiden, dressed in graveclothes. Instantly because of the inrush of air, the body dissolved into a cloud of yellow dust. One of the explorers walked over to the ledge and brushing his hand along it gathered up in one hand all that had been the body of a human being—just one handful of dust.

Who could believe that this handful of dust had ever lived and loved, suffered and enjoyed, that once it had assumed the form of a human being and perhaps had stood out in the open night looking up in wonderment at the heavens, that it had clothed the personality of a young woman who lifted hands of prayer to God? Just a handful of dust! Yes, but a handful of dust infused with the divine Spirit—the breath of God.

The accumulated evidence would seem to indicate that man's body and brain are instruments for the use of his mind—or self or soul. Years ago William James suggested this thought. It may well be, he declared, that the relation of the brain to the self is transmissive rather than creative. "The phenomena of consciousness," he wrote, "may imply not the production but the transmission of mind by brain."

In that case we shall have to change the illustration the materialists used. The relation of man's brain to his intelligent self is not that of music to the harp in such a manner that if the harp be destroyed, the music ceases. His self or soul is the *harpist* rather than the music. If his harp should be destroyed, he will find another on which to express the music of his soul.

I doubt if this argument has ever been more convincingly expressed than in the words of J. Ellis McTaggart, who employed a strikingly original figure of speech. He writes:

If a man is shut up in a house, the transparency of the windows is an essential condition of his seeing the sky. But it would not be prudent to infer that if he walked out of the house, he could not see the sky because there was no longer any glass through which he might see it.

It is important to remember that in our discussion of the relation between body and soul we have not attempted to produce a "proof" of immortality. We have merely reversed the analogy that materialists have employed to discredit belief in everlasting life. In doing this, we have cleared the way for other evidence that may be presented for the life everlasting.

## The possibility of reunion

Eternal life would not be a fully satisfying experience for most of us if we could not know the joy of reunion and fellowship with those who have gone before us. But how can we hope for such an experience? A stumbling block for many is the thought of the years that will have passed since we said farewell to our loved ones. How shall we be able to recognize them after we have been separated from them for twenty, forty, or even eighty years? This raises a further question: What will be the basis of this recognition? Will it be entirely or even largely physical? Wouldn't the changes of the passing years make identification impossible? The years do take their toll of a man. His face becomes wrinkled, his hair white, his body bent, his step slow, and his memory defective. The buoyancy and vigor of his youth disappear. The tenement in which man's spirit lives becomes dilapidated with age. Yet man's ability to recognize another need not be affected if it be a faculty of the soul as well as of the body. Even in this life isn't the basis of recognition oftentimes as much spiritual as physical? The soul is ageless and timeless. It becomes richer in knowledge and insight as the years go by, until at last it bursts through its restraining walls of clay.

Edward Everett Hale, the noted New England preacher and author of the last century, wrote some sixty books, was editor of a number of journals, and widely known as a speaker. At eighty-one he was made chaplain of the United States Senate. He died in Boston at the ripe old age of eighty-seven. When his friends met him on the street, near the close of his life, they would ask, "How is Mr. Hale today?" The old man, tapping his way along the sidewalk, would reply, "Mr. Hale is very well. The old tenement he is living in is getting pretty shaky now, and it won't be long until Mr. Hale will be leaving it, but he is very well himself, thank you, very well indeed."

## The survival of whole personalities

The New Testament describes the body as a dwelling that we must vacate, as a tent that we must abandon, and as a garment that one day we shall put off forever. Perhaps it would be more accurate to say that we exchange our earthly tent for a heavenly one. An allowable translation of II Cor. 5:4 would read: "I groan within this tent of mine, being heavily burdened; not that I long to put this tent off, but to put on the other over it, so that my mortality may be swallowed up in life."

Paul here sets forth his concept of a spiritual body with which the soul will be clothed in the resurrection. Neither the New Testament nor of course Paul suggests that in the experience of immortality body and soul are separated and the body has no part or lot in it. That is Plato's view, and seems to promise only a fragmented personality in the afterlife, though the Greek philosopher felt that it was the most precious element in man that was preserved. At the same time the New Testament goes beyond the Hebrew standpoint of the resurrection or resuscitation of the flesh. Neither of these concepts satisfied Paul nor ought to satisfy us. A disembodied soul would not meet the requirements of a continuing personality. In II Cor. 5:3, Paul writes that if our earthly body (or tent) be taken down, God will supply us with another or a new body. When the soul is clothed in this new or spiritual body "we shall not be found naked." Again, the Apostle says of the soul, "God giveth it a body as it hath pleased him." And once more, "There is a natural body, and there is a spiritual body."

This Pauline concept is far removed from the viewpoint of Thomas Aquinas, who argues that we are justified "in believing that our fleshly bodies rise and remain fleshly, animal and material throughout everlasting life." "Flesh and blood cannot inherit the kingdom of God," says Paul.

Any attempts to depict the exact nature of life in the "world to come" are mere flights of imagination. It must suffice us to know that the New Testament promises us a full personal life with powers of communication of person with person. So we may hope for endowments far more perfect and more adapted to a spiritual existence than any material body could ever be.

Meanwhile in this present life we are dependent on a physical body that is subject to all the ravages of time. Memory and intellect begin to fail as we get older because the brain cells are aging. The instrument used by the "self" has deteriorated, and it must find another. When we believe that personal identity survives death, we affirm that memory and affection and love also live on. Thus death loses its terror for the Christian and becomes the open door to a glorious adventure.

## Awareness of the unseen

The Epistle to the Hebrews contains a sentence that graphically portrays in symbolic language the world of the unseen: "Wherefore seeing we also are compassed about with so great a cloud of witnesses." The author of this sentence was thinking in terms of the amphitheaters that were found in cities throughout the Roman Empire. Tier upon tier of circling benches rose above the sands of the arena, where trained athletes and gladiators struggled for mastery. These contenders, looking up, could see thousands of faces like a luminous cloud—the faces of the spectators watching them and urging them on.

In the heavenly amphitheater the author of this epistle visualizes the heroes of the faith, whose names he proudly recalls in the eleventh chapter. Doubtless among them were friends and comrades and loved ones. It is these that make up the "great cloud of witnesses."

Perhaps an illustration will make clear what I mean. J. Paterson-Smyth, who has written with such understanding on the theme of immortality, tells the story of a young lad in one of the historic schools of England. This boy was the best cricket player in the school. His father was blind, but he always attended the cricket matches. He could not see his son play, but he thrilled to hear his son's name called by the spectators. Then came a day during the school term when the father died. One of the principal matches of the season was to come off the day after the funeral. The school team was sure to be beaten without its ablest player. To the surprise of everyone he suddenly appeared in the dressing room. Never had the students or teachers seen him play so well. He saved the day for his team. Afterward his captain said to him, "We scarcely hoped that you would be with us since your father was buried only yesterday."

"Well, you see," said the boy, "I had to do my best since this was the first time my father ever saw me play."

"Seeing we also are compassed about with so great a cloud of witnesses."

The Greek word for "witnesses" doesn't mean just onlookers. It means also those who testify or give warning. The writer is suggesting that we are surrounded by those who have passed from our sight but they are not indifferent to our conflicts and struggles. They are watching us and urging us on to victory.

This picture of the world of the unseen agrees in every way with the teachings of the Bible in both the Old and New Testaments. The servant of Elisha was overcome with fear at the sight of a great body of the enemy surrounding them, but the dauntless prophet prayed, "Lord, I pray thee, open his eyes, that he may see." The Lord opened the eyes of the young man, and he saw that the mountain was filled with horses and chariots of fire around Elisha. Isaiah at prayer in the temple had a spiritual vision. He saw the Lord seated on a throne in majesty, his glory filling the temple. In Bethlehem on the night of our Saviour's birth the hosts of heaven made the earth echo and re-echo with their hymns of rejoicing. On the Mount of Transfiguration the wondering disciples saw Moses and Elijah appear, talking with Christ. Stephen, doomed to the cruel death of a martyr, looked up to heaven and cried, "I see the heavens opened, and the Son of man standing on the right hand of God." Saul on the road to Damascus had a vision of the risen, exalted Christ.

It is nowhere suggested in the Bible that the eternal world is located in some far-off corner of the universe, but rather that it is very near at hand. It requires only the drawing aside of a veil for the eyes of faith to behold its glories. It would be difficult therefore to find a truer symbolism than that contained in the words, "Wherefore seeing we also are compassed about with so great a cloud of witnesses."

## Scientific analogies

Many of the facts made known by science point quite definitely to a world of the unseen. The physicists, for instance, have done a great deal of research in the field of sound and sight. We are told that the lowest sound we can hear has a frequency of thirty-two waves per second. The highest has 32,000 waves per second. There are many sounds on either end of these wave lengths that we do not hear. Indeed, it has been shown that animals and insects hear sounds that man does not. The physicists also tell us that sound does not really exist but only sound waves. Briefly this is how the phenomenon of the human voice over the radio is explained. The speaker's vocal cords set up certain vibrations. These vibrations produce sound waves in the air that are caught up by the microphone and changed into electric waves. The electric waves are again cast upon the air. They spread out in widening circles like the ripples of water when a stone is dropped into a pond. These vibrations are caught up by a receiving set and transmitted in the form of sound waves to the air. Finally they vibrate on the eardrums of the person listening to the radio, and are communicated to his brain.

We cannot help wondering what sounds we should hear were we tuned in to lower and higher frequencies than now reach us. If we went out in the early dawn some summer's day, when God is about to remake his world, would we hear the "morning stars sing together and all the sons of God shout for joy"?

Similarly, the human brain interprets certain wave

lengths that fall upon the retina of our eyes to give us sight. Our vision is limited to electromagnetic waves of a certain length. A scientific writer once put it like this: If you were to set sixty pianos end to end to represent the whole range of vibrations that exist in space, one piano out of the sixty would represent the number of vibrations a human being receives. In other words, there are many more vibrations in the ether around us than we have the power to hear or see. What an amazing universe we inhabit! We should always be careful never to think that anything that our senses cannot detect is worthless or trivial. Sir Arthur Eddington, one of the greatest scientists of this century, freely admitted that there is as much truth in the religious interpretation of supraphysical energy—energy beyond and above the physical—as in the scientific.

What might we not see with our eyes if they had the gift of spiritual vision? Would we see that great cloud of witnesses who recognize us, who speak our names, who are eagerly watching from the battlements of the eternal kingdom? The words "a great cloud of witnesses" remind us of some of the paintings of Raphael. Often the backgrounds of his masterpieces are clouds of bright mist. When we examine these clouds more closely, we see that they are composed of hosts of calm, sweet, angelic faces. The idea of a spiritual kingdom surrounding us was never far from the mind of Raphael.

## Further thoughts on reunion

Fundamental to our belief in immortality is our hope of reunion with those who have gone before. Indeed, eternal life would be without its deepest joys if love were to be deprived of its dearest object. F. H. Bradley, in his philosophic study *Appearance and Reality,* affirms that this "appeal to the affections," this "desire to meet once more those whom we have loved," is "the only appeal as to the future life which to me individually is not hollow." It is easy enough to think of the arguments that stand in the way of such a belief: the man whose father and mother died when he was a little child, the aging parents who lost a baby in their youth, the people whom death has separated for scores of years. But all these arguments overlook a vital point. As we have indicated earlier in this chapter, even in this present life recognition is not basically physical. The thing that makes us different from one another and from every human creature that will ever be born is not physical so much as spiritual. The deepest recognition comes through what we cannot touch or actually see, the thing called personality. It can be made despite the physical toll of swiftly passing years.

From time to time we read of a son who left home in his early teens to seek his fortune. Past middle age he returns to visit a mother who is old and frail. The physical resemblance of each of them has completely changed in the intervening half a century. Yet when they come into each other's presence, soul leaps forth to greet soul. Writing of such an experience, the poet Momerie makes the returning son say,

> It was not mother that I knew thy face;
> It was my heart that cried out Mother!

## The cult of Spiritualism

It is easy to understand that bereaved persons should yearn for a physical sign or word that those they love still live beyond death. After each world war people became greatly interested in spiritualism. In cities all over the world séances flourished.

More than twenty years ago I spent several hours a week for an entire winter studying spiritualism. A well-known physician, whose contributions on this theme have been published in American magazines, was director of these investigations. Fourteen cameras were set up in the séance room. When an operator pushed a single button, flash bulbs lighted up the room and fourteen simultaneous pictures were taken. At the end of a winter's study I was compelled to confess that no tangible results had been achieved. Some of the findings were wholly disappointing.

One night, according to a medium, the spirit of Charles Haddon Spurgeon appeared and talked with me. Evidently his intellectual gifts had sadly deteriorated. When I asked him a question about the Bible, he stammered his ignorance.

Occasionally, too, we are revolted by such happenings as the one alleged to have occurred at a séance in Boston. A group of ministers were assembled for a demonstration. The spirit of Phillips Brooks appeared, and out of the darkness the great preacher addressed his colleagues in these words: "How are you fellows out there?"

A. E. Taylor, late professor of moral philosophy at Edinburgh University, speaks caustically of some of the "revelations" produced even by celebrated spiritualists:

We are expected to believe that the heroic dead derive their happiness from the consumption of spectral whiskies and sodas, and the smoking of ghostly cigars. . . . This and how much more of it there is all round us is worse than childishness; it is vulgar-minded worldliness.

Nevertheless, on the subject of spiritualism and extrasensory perception, we must continue to keep an open mind. The rejection of certain aspects of these subjects and the actual detection of fraud does not necessarily prove that the whole subject is valueless.

The New Testament represents eternal life as a social experience. What possible blessing could it confer if it were but a solitary experience with isolated souls wandering forever in loneliness? We believe that consciousness, memory, character, and personal identity live on. And the Bible encourages our faith. These demand a relationship with others to give them meaning and expression. One of the tenderest incidents in the life of our Lord was that in which he assured the penitent thief on the cross, "Today shalt thou be with me in paradise." How this promise, given with divine authority, must have altered the penitent thief's attitude toward death! Now he knows that he has found a Friend who would meet him and welcome him into the heavenly kingdom, and appoint for him a place in his Father's house on high. In moments of deepest Christian insight we see that eternal life carries with it the assurance of a heavenly companionship. It conveys a pledge of fellowship with God and with the great cloud of witnesses who are never far from us. We witness to all this when we affirm in the words of the Apostle's Creed: "I believe in . . . the communion of saints."

## Glimpses beyond the veil

In the biographies of great Christians we often read that, in the closing moments of their lives, they apparently became aware of the proximity and reality of the world to come. Sometimes they caught glimpses of those whom they had "loved long since, and lost awhile." In North-

67

field, Massachusetts, a group of ministers once stood on what is known as "Round Top," a lovely bit of ground where Dwight L. Moody is buried. We recalled how in the closing years of his life he was made lonely by the death, within a year, of his grandson, little Dwight, and his granddaughter, Irene. Later came death's summons to the great evangelist himself. His son, Will Moody, says that as he lay on his deathbed with his eyes closed and almost unconscious, suddenly his face lighted up with rapture and he cried, "Dwight, Irene, I can see the children's faces!"

How fitting that little children, whom he loved so dearly, should lead him into that land of light and joy where every broken fellowship is renewed and he would hear the Master say, "Well done, good and faithful servant . . . enter thou into the joy of thy lord." The fact that a man believes in an immortal life that begins in the present and goes on without interruption into eternity will more than any other incentive inspire him to live at his best. As Franklin K. Lane expressed it in one of his letters:

The only miracle I care about is the resurrection. If we live again, we certainly have reason for living now. I think that belief is the foundation hope of Christianity.

This belief emphasizes also the dignity and worth of man's personality. Men and women, made in the image of God, are the heirs of eternal life. When we believe that each man's personality survives death, and that memory, affection, and love live on in a fully conscious existence, death no longer inspires terror. It becomes an open door to a glorious adventure. It leads us into new experiences of service and worship, new disciplines, and ever deepening joys.

During the year 1927, while fulfilling the conditions

of a travel scholarship, I had the privilege of hearing many preachers in Great Britain. No voice was more prophetic than that of Arthur Hird, who preached for Dr. Norwood in the City Temple, London. The church was packed to the doors every Sunday. Many people were turned away. On several occasions Hird preached on eternity and its influence on life here and now. This is what he said: "To me eternal life means worship, adoration, and the challenge of fresh errands in God's service, and the acceptance of even larger tasks."

At the beginning of 1932, Hird said, "I find myself strangely on tiptoe as I enter 1932." Quite unexpectedly, before a month had passed, God called him. A friend who had listened to his prophetic words wrote:

Good-bye, Arthur Hird, brave soul, valiant warrior, good-bye for now. You were strangely on tiptoe when you entered the year. You did not know that you were about to meet the glad surprise that awaits the good and faithful servant.

A Christian will meet death unafraid. This was the spirit in which Charles Frohman, the American theatrical producer, met man's last enemy. As the "Lusitania" was plowing her way through the Atlantic toward Britain in May, 1915, there were many anxious hearts on board because of the public warning that she would be torpedoed. Finally word reached the passengers that they were nearing their destination. Feelings of tension relaxed.

But suddenly a periscope rose above the waves, and a torpedo rushed toward the side of the ship, striking it with a sickening crash. Then came panic and a rush for the lifeboats. Charles Frohman was standing by the rail of the ship. A passenger on his way to a lifeboat passed him.

Looking at Frohman's peaceful face, he asked, "Aren't you afraid?"

"Afraid?" answered Frohman. "No. Why fear death? It is the most beautiful adventure of life."

Anyone who truly believes in eternal life as proclaimed by Jesus Christ will face the experience of death unafraid.

## Immortality is not inaction

Some object to the Christian doctrine of immortality on the ground that it puts too much emphasis on everlasting rest. Unfortunately, quite a few Christians still think of heaven as a place of complete inaction. Yet such a concept is far removed from true restfulness. William Cowper wrote:

> Absence of occupation is not rest,
> A mind quite vacant is a mind distress'd.

Many of the most restless and unhappy people in the world are those who have nothing to do. Everyone engaged in work that he enjoys knows the feeling of complete restfulness that comes when he is most busy.

John Greenleaf Whittier combats the idea of heaven as a place of endless rest. In his poem "The Dying Monk" he tells of one who visits the deathbed of a fellow monk and offers comfort. He tells the sick man to remember that everlasting rest and a crown of gold are awaiting him. But the monk replies that such rewards are not for him. The crown would be too heavy for his poor, old, gray head. He cannot endure the thought that his hands, calloused by toil for others, should soon be folded in unceasing rest. He asks if death will so change him that he will become indifferent to the needs of others. The visitor is shocked by what seems to him to be stark rebellion, and he flees

from the room. But there comes to the dying man the voice
of the Lord saying,

> Tender and most compassionate, never fear;
> Heaven is love and God himself is love,
> Thy work below shall be thy work above.

Whatever justification Whittier needed for the message of
his poem may be found in an unforgettable verse of the
New Testament. In the Revelation we read: "His servants
shall serve him: And they shall see his face." The Bible
does not hold before us in the future life the expectation
of complete repose, idleness, and apathy. It promises,
rather, the true rest of loving service.

Our Lord illustrates one phase of the heavenly life by
his parable of the talents. An Oriental monarch returning
from a long journey requires his servants to give an
account of their stewardship while he was absent. He
recompenses those who had made faithful use of the
talents entrusted to them. But the reward is not a promise
that now all their labors are ended. He promises them
larger opportunities of service.

> Well done, thou good and faithful servant: thou hast been
> faithful over a few things, I will make thee ruler over many
> things: enter thou into the joy of thy lord.

These words of our Lord bring to mind the thirtieth
anniversary sermon preached by Charles E. Jefferson at the
Broadway Tabernacle, New York. He remarked to his
congregation that he hadn't the slightest anxiety lest he
run out of sermon material:

Rather I am now haunted by the fear that I shall not have time to preach all the sermons that are in me. My sermonic stock is so enormous that only eternity can give me a chance to use it. I see clearly that I have got to keep on preaching in the next world. I hope the Broadway Tabernacle will be there, and that it will give me a call. I should love to be the pastor of the Tabernacle for thirty thousand years. Think of writing a thirty thousandth anniversary sermon!

Such thoughts come often into the minds of ministers who love to preach. Indeed, it is their secret hope that they may be called upon to address congregations vastly larger than even radio or television can command. Just as long as there are souls who, in this life, have never known Christ or his gospel, who need to be led and instructed and delivered from the bondage of ignorance and fear, just so long will God's servants have opportunity to serve him. In the divine presence our highest glory will not be achieved in idleness, but in laboring for Him whose service is perfect freedom and perfect rest.

# CHAPTER FIVE

# THE POWER
# OF THE RESURRECTION

JOSEPH FORT NEWTON IN HIS AUTOBIOGRAPHY *River of Years* tells of a day when for the first time he looked into an open grave. He was a young lad when his father died. At the funeral, on a snowy, gloomy day, he stood beside the grave, gripping his mother's hand. It seemed to him as though the bottom had dropped out of his world. In this moment of utter loneliness the kindly old country minister began to read the burial service: "I am the resurrection, and the life: he that believeth in me, though he were dead, yet shall he live; and whosoever liveth and believeth in me shall never die."

"Never shall I forget the thrill of those words," writes Newton. "It was as if a great hand, stronger than the hand of a man and gentler than the hand of a woman, had reached out from the unseen to touch and to heal. From that day to this," he concludes, "I have loved Jesus to distraction."

Tens of thousands of brokenhearted men and women have experienced this same healing touch of Christ as they have listened to the words "I am the resurrection, and the life." For millions of Christian men and women the keystone of their faith in everlasting life is the resurrection of Jesus Christ. As our Lord said, "Because I live, ye shall live also."

The resurrection of Christ is the heart, the core, the inner citadel, of the Christian faith. It gives importance to every other belief about our Lord. Christianity stands or falls by the Resurrection.

The evidence cited by Christians for the resurrection of Christ may be summed up as follows:

First: There is the New Testament witness of the empty tomb. Some have asserted that our Christian faith in the Resurrection rests on an empty tomb. This is not accurate. It rests, rather, on the living Christ and his manifestation in history and the life of man. Yet the fact of the empty tomb is not to be taken lightly. All four evangelists assert that the grave was empty on the morning of the resurrection.

## Critical theories of the Resurrection

Critical writers of the nineteenth and early twentieth centuries set forth theories of the Resurrection that cast doubt on the evidence for the empty tomb. These are known as the fraud theory, the swoon theory, and the vision theory.

The fraud theory suggested that the disciples of Jesus deliberately falsified the evidence. The swoon theory implied that he did not actually die on the cross, but only swooned and was resuscitated by the coolness of the tomb. The vision theory declared that the basis of the resurrection stories was a vision of Christ seen by one or more of the disciples.

The swoon theory might be more accurately described as the resuscitation theory. Schleiermacher was one of those who suggested that Jesus had swooned in agony and had revived in the tomb. Heinrich E. G. Paulus, the German theologian and champion of rationalism, greatly elabo-

74

rated the resuscitation theory. Every now and then someone even in our own time presents this theory, not knowing that it had been argued with considerable skill in the
nineteenth century. For instance, a little time ago I received a letter from an American physician who is an able
and kindly man. The approach of Easter led him to write
that he could not accept literally the New Testament account of the resurrection of Jesus. He offered this alterna-
tive:

It has always been my belief that Jesus had fainted on the
cross instead of dying, and when Joseph of Arimathea put Him
in his own vault, the coolness and rest brought Him around.
And then possibly with Joseph's help He escaped and was
hidden from the authorities but was seen later, on various
occasions, by His disciples who, quite naturally, having thought
He had died, believed that He had returned from heaven.

This doctor did not know that his theory was but a
brief restatement of the views of Schleiermacher and
Paulus. The theory when elaborated last century was given
a deathblow from an unexpected quarter. The German
theologian and philosopher David Friedrich Strauss, who
was the proclaimed enemy of supernaturalism and who had
attempted to prove that Bible history is mythical, nevertheless was constrained to say of the resuscitation theory:

It is impossible that a being who had stolen half-dead out
of the sepulchre, who crept about weak and ill, wanting medical treatment, who required bandaging, strengthening, and
indulgence, and who still at last yielded to his sufferings,
could have given to the disciples the impression that he was a
Conqueror over death and the grave, the Prince of Life, an
impression which lay at the bottom of their future ministry.

The vision theory was built on the belief that the disciples and friends of Jesus confidently expected his resurrection. Yet the reverse of this appears to be true. The Gospels declare that the women had gone to the tomb to embalm Jesus' body. This indicates that they expected him to remain in the grave. Did not even his most intimate disciples find it hard to believe the early reports of his resurrection? We also have Paul's statement that the risen Christ had appeared to five hundred people at one time. It would be an extraordinary circumstance that would produce the same illusion in such a large number of people.

## The disciples before the Sanhedrin

If the high priests and members of the Sanhedrin believed that the body of Jesus still lay in its tomb in Joseph's garden, why did they fail to mention this fact or to produce some evidence of it? When Peter and John were on trial before the Sanhedrin, only seven weeks after the Resurrection, an unparalleled opportunity was afforded the religious authorities to discredit the disciples' claim of a resurrection.

And it came to pass on the morrow, that their rulers, and elders, and scribes, and Annas the high priest, and Caiaphas, and John, and Alexander, and as many as were of the kindred of the high priest, were gathered together at Jerusalem. And when they had set them in the midst, they asked, By what power, or by what name, have ye done this? Then Peter, filled with the Holy Ghost, said unto them, Ye rulers of the people, and elders of Israel, If we this day be examined of the good deed done to the impotent man, by what means he is made whole; be it known unto you all, and to all the people of Israel, that by the name of Jesus Christ of Nazareth, whom ye crucified, whom God raised from the dead, even by him doth this man stand here before you whole.

So far as the records go, no single word of rebuttal was offered by the Sanhedrin.

Those who would deny the authenticity of the empty tomb are on the horns of a dilemma. Either Jesus' enemies possessed his body or knew where it was, or else his followers had hidden it away. The first possibility is ruled out by the silence of the Sanhedrinists. If the second were true, then all the apostolic sermons and affirmations about the resurrection of Jesus are founded on the most gigantic fraud in human history. Likewise, we should have to believe that the apostles gladly became martyrs to perpetuate a hoax. Was it not Tertullian who said that men do not willingly die for a cause unless they know it is the truth? We are left with the conclusion that the resurrection stories of the New Testament present a substantially accurate account of the events that followed the death of our Lord on the cross.

## The gospel of the Resurrection

Second: We have the impressive evidence that the central theme of all the apostolic preaching was the resurrection of their Lord and Master. In Acts 4:1-2 we read:

And as they spake unto the people, the priests, and the captain of the temple, and the Sadducees, came upon them, being grieved that they taught the people, and preached through Jesus the resurrection from the dead.

In the same chapter we read in verse thirty-three: "And with great power gave the apostles witness of the resurrection of the Lord Jesus: and great grace was upon them all."

The importance that was laid upon the preaching and witness to the resurrection of Jesus is emphasized in Acts 1:21-22. Peter pointed out to the disciples that following the defection and death of Judas. it was necessary that a disciple be chosen to take his place. This is how he expressed it:

Wherefore of these men which have companied with us all the time that the Lord Jesus went in and out among us, beginning from the baptism of John, unto that same day that he was taken up from us, must one be ordained to be a witness with us of his resurrection.

The most important consideration in the choice of this disciple was the fact that he had accompanied the disciples and the Lord throughout his ministry and had witnessed his resurrection from the dead.

With the coming of Pentecost, a new and powerful impetus was given to the witness of the apostles. And Peter standing with the other eleven preached the first sermon after the descent of the Holy Spirit. Central in this sermon, which doubtless set the keynote for much of the apostolic preaching, was Peter's deliverance when he said:

Ye men of Israel, hear these words; Jesus of Nazareth, a man approved of God among you by miracles and wonders and signs, which God did by him in the midst of you, as ye yourselves also know: Him, being delivered by the determinate counsel and foreknowledge of God, ye have taken, and by wicked hands have crucified and slain: whom God hath raised up, having loosed the pains of death: because it was not possible that he should be holden of it.

Throughout the apostolic writings the resurrection of

Jesus Christ formed the very substance of Christian doctrine. Indeed it was this preaching that won converts to the Church and built it up from strength to strength.

Third: We have the witness of Paul. The conversion of Saul of Tarsus is one of the most powerful confirmations of the Resurrection contained in the New Testament. He had been one of the bitterest opponents of Christianity. In after years he wrote to the Galatians: "For you have heard of my former life in Judaism, how I persecuted the church of God violently and tried to destroy it." And to Timothy he wrote: "Who was before a blasphemer, and a persecutor, and injurious: but I obtained mercy, because I did it ignorantly in unbelief."

From this state of hostility toward Christianity Paul suddenly came into complete certainty through his confrontation with the risen Christ on the road to Damascus. Our Lord appeared to him in the power and glory of the life everlasting. From that moment Saul of Tarsus became a changed man. The persecutor was transformed into an apostle. His living Lord was the mainspring of all his faith and the source of all his power. The resurrection was the central theme of his preaching. He emphasizes this fact in his second letter to Timothy: "Remember that Jesus Christ of the seed of David was raised from the dead, according to my gospel."

Here we have incontrovertible evidence of a powerful inward transformation in the apostle Paul. Some twenty-five years later he wrote what is probably the most authoritative single statement on the Resurrection that appears in the New Testament. It is considerably older than the Gospels.

For I delivered unto you first of all that which I also received, how that Christ died for our sins according to the scriptures; and that he was buried, and that he rose again the third day according to the scriptures: and that he was seen of Cephas, then of the twelve: after that, he was seen of above five hundred brethren at once; of whom the greater part remain unto this present, but some are fallen asleep. After that, he was seen of James; then of all the apostles.

Fourth: We have the indirect evidence of many people from all walks of life. These people testified to the signs and wonders wrought in the name of the risen Christ. A surging joy that opposition could not quench filled the hearts of those who believed in him. It gave significance to the lives of multitudes of people formerly regarded as unimportant. All over the Roman Empire were little colonies of believers in the risen, living Christ who rejoiced that they were "counted worthy to suffer shame for his name." So mighty was the impact of this gospel of the Resurrection that scarcely three centuries had passed before the Cross of the Galilean had triumphed over the Roman eagles.

Fifth: There is the evidence of Jesus' own teaching that he confidently expected his resurrection. With the approach of death he showed no fear that his influence over his followers would lessen. Indeed he declared that after the Resurrection his disciples would do even more mighty deeds because of the power that would flow from him in his resurrected life.

Jesus' confidence in the continuation of his influence is in striking contrast to the attitude of some other religious leaders. Confucius is a case in point. A note of optimism flowed naturally through his philosophy. Yet as death approached, he began to lose heart. His own faith burned low. The prospect of the future filled him with foreboding. He said, "My principles make no progress, and I? How shall I be viewed in future ages?" These sentiments are poles removed from the spirit of our Lord who declared, "Heaven and earth shall pass away, but my words shall not pass away." It was faith in the Resurrection that made all the difference.

Arnold Toynbee reminded us of the centrality of Christ's resurrection when, in *A Study of History,* he wrote:

The One remains, the many change and pass. And this is in truth the final result of our survey of saviours. When we set out on this quest we found ourselves moving in the midst of a mighty host, but, as we have pressed forward, the marchers, company by company, have fallen out of the race. . . . At the final ordeal of death, few, even of these would-be saviour gods, have dared to put their title to the test by plunging into the icy river. And now, as we stand and gaze with our eyes fixed upon the farther shore, a single figure rises from the flood and straightway fills the whole horizon. There is the Saviour; "and the pleasure of the Lord shall prosper in his hand; he shall see of the travail of his soul and shall be satisfied."

Before Jesus plunged "into the icy river," he calmly predicted that he would triumph over death and the grave.

## The disciples transformed

Sixth: Of great importance is the complete transformation wrought in the disciples by the knowledge that death could not hold their Master. Without exception they became changed men. This is a powerful psychological argument for the Resurrection.

Stainer's *Crucifixion,* which is so often sung on Good Friday, ends with these words: "And he bowed his head and gave up the ghost." Stainer's intention was to leave the listener in gloomy suspense with no hint of a coming dawn. Easter, on the other hand, is a festival of joy, of hope, of life. There is but one day between earth's saddest day and gladdest day.

The death of Jesus plunged his disciples into deepest despair. It quenched all their hopes. For eleven men the world had come to an end. The stars were blotted out of their sky. Night descended on their souls. They had expected to see the Master ascend a throne. Instead they saw him nailed to a cross. They had come to believe that the whole nation would give him its allegiance. But instead they heard the mob crying, "Away with him, crucify him!" They saw heaped upon him every indignity, every torture, every shame, that the twisted brains of cruel men could devise. He died a death reserved for slaves and revolutionists.

This was the end of their dream. Their Master had become "a poor broken-down thing, dead on the cross." Here was a tragedy so deep and dark that they could see in it no purpose and beyond it no ray of hope. Evil had proved stronger than good. Hate had defeated love. Wrong had worsted right. Injustice had finally triumphed. They had given their glad allegiance to a holy cause that was now irretrievably lost.

When Caiaphas laid his head on his pillow the night of the Crucifixion, he was content. The troublesome Galilean had been disposed of at last. And Pilate? Well, had he not publicly washed his hands of the whole affair? Anyway it was now a dead issue.

## The death of Jesus was no closed case

In the movie *The Life of Zola* there is a remarkable court scene. Zola was battling to reopen the Dreyfus affair, but his evidence was not admitted and his witnesses were not allowed to testify. Finally the judge declared that it was a closed case. As they were leaving the courtroom, Zola's lawyer pointed to a mural above the judge's head. It was a painting of the Crucifixion. The lawyer said, "That, too, was once regarded as 'a closed case.'"

That "closed case" of nineteen centuries ago was opened by the hand of the Eternal. God manifested his limitless power in the resurrection of his Son, who stepped forth from the shadows of the tomb in the power of an endless life. The disciples became new men. Cowards were changed into heroes; pygmies became giants; broken reeds pillars of iron. This is how Walter Russell Bowie described the miraculous happenings:

These men, so helpless, so empty-hearted, so broken on the day of the crucifixion, became transformed, every one of them. They moved with confidence in a recreated world. They knew that Jesus was stronger than those who had attempted to silence Him. He was alive. He would live in them, and they would go forth adventurously to conquer new worlds.

What but the resurrection of their Lord in divine power could have lifted these men from floundering defeat into the certitude of victory?

## The Christian Church emerges

Seventh: the existence of a Christian Church. We require the Resurrection to account for the presence of the Church in the world.

The resurrection of Jesus Christ is the cornerstone of the Christian faith. Without it there would have been no Church, no holy Scripture, no radiant message of One who triumphed over sin and death. Even as Phidias, the Greek sculptor, interwove his name in the shield of

Minerva so that it could not be removed without destroying the shield, so is the resurrection of Jesus Christ in the Gospels. Remove the Easter story from the New Testament and its total structure is destroyed. "Christ is risen" still remains the best of all good news which the Church proclaims.

The change from the age-old institution of the Jewish Sabbath celebrated on Saturday to the Lord's Day, known nowadays as Sunday, is a continuing historical memorial of the Resurrection and a powerful confirmation of its reality. The Lord's Supper, with its note of triumphant joy, has ever witnessed to the fact that it is not a sacramental celebration to the memory of a dead Jesus. It is a joyous recognition of him who is "alive for evermore."

Eighth: There is the experience of the living Christ in the hearts of men. Nowhere in the New Testament is Christ presented merely as a fact of history—a great and good man who has given to the world moral and spiritual principles which will influence mankind to the end of time. Nor is he made simply an affirmation of the Christian creed. Always Jesus Christ is set forth by the apostles as a reality to be experienced, as a living presence in the world about them, as a transforming power in their lives.

Paul, especially, is the exponent of the living Christ. There would be no gain in trying to discover under what form Christ appeared to him on the road to Damascus or how his words touched Paul's consciousness. But one fact is established beyond doubt: the apostle saw the Lord, he heard the Lord, he spoke with the Lord, and throughout his entire life his faith in the reality of this experience never wavered. Indeed it deepened as the years passed because of the continuous fellowship Paul maintained with the risen, living Christ. So he could write: "Therefore if any man be in Christ, he is a new creature." "I live; yet not I, but Christ liveth in me." "I can do all things through Christ which strengtheneth me." The most real fact in the world for Paul was not the Jesus of history but the Christ of experience with whom he daily walked and talked.

This was true of all the apostles. They believed that the spirit of Christ dwelt in them and that his divine power was manifested through them. Even more wonderful is the fact that throughout nineteen centuries of Christian history the risen Christ has continued to empower and guide men and women. The difference between these persons and Paul is only one of degree. Matthew Arnold wrote: "Paul's conversion is for science an event of precisely the same nature as the conversion of which the history of Methodism relates so many."

We need only read the biographies of great Christians in every century to see the powerful influence of our Lord on the heroes of our faith. So many illustrations come to mind that we are embarrassed by their abundance. Witness the faith of such men as Francis of Assisi in his intimate spiritual friendship with Christ, Phillips Brooks, to whom our Lord was as real as the members of his own household, and David Livingstone of Africa, who made this entry in his diary concerning Christ's promise that he would be with us always: "It is the word of a Gentleman of the most strict and sacred honor." All this is equally true of multitudes of humble Christian men and women whose names will never be recorded in history. They, too, knew Christ in loving fellowship.

The New Testament does not argue from a general resurrection to the resurrection of our Lord. The argument is always the other way around. "But in fact Christ has been raised from the dead, the first fruits of those who have fallen asleep. . . . For as in Adam all die, so also in Christ shall all be made alive." "God hath both raised up the Lord, and will raise up us by his own power." The Church's faith in the resurrection of Jesus was a supreme expression of its trust in almighty God. There is not the slightest doubt that the secret of the martyrs' courage lay in their belief that death would usher them into the presence of their crucified but exalted Lord.

## On being sure of resurrection

Once men have conquered the fear of death, they can face anything that life may have in store for them. A young American lad, who was wounded in World War II and returned to this country in 1945, related a happening that illustrates this truth. A soldier lay wounded on the battlefield. He had been given up for dead. As life slowly came back to him, he thirsted for water. There was no one to dress his wounds, and he lay out in the open field from Good Friday until Easter morning. When allied planes passed overhead, he tried to sit up or wave his arms to attract attention. Constantly he prayed for relief from pain and from the raging thirst that tortured him. Mercifully he slipped off into unconsciousness.

He awoke in a hospital bed with a chaplain bending over him.

"You say, my boy, that you were wounded on Good Friday and that you have been lying on the battlefield ever since," said the chaplain. "Do you know that this is Easter morning?"

The lad answered, "How wonderful! For me, too, it is like a resurrection. Out there on the field I died a thousand deaths, but *somehow we do not mind the crucifixion when we are sure of the resurrection.*"

Now perhaps we can better understand the meaning of Paul's triumphant cry, "Thanks be to God, which giveth us the victory through our Lord Jesus Christ."

CHAPTER SIX

# A PERSONAL CONFESSION
# OF FAITH

RALPH WALDO EMERSON SAYS THAT MOST PEOPLE who discuss the subject of immortality begin at once to quote the views of others. I suppose this is natural because all of us desire to reflect on the hopes and convictions of the best minds of the race as they have grappled with the problem of life and death. For myself, one of the strongest bulwarks of faith in eternal life is the profound impact that Jesus Christ has made on human history. Other great men have walked our earth and have gained the allegiance of many people, but none other has influenced the course of human history so powerfully as has our Lord. His stature grows not less but more as the centuries pass.

We see this truth more clearly as we compare Jesus with another noble character of history. Socrates is a case in point. The circumstances of his death are worth recounting. In the year 399 B.C., a group of men were seated around their leader in a death cell of an Athens prison. He had been condemned on a charge of disbelieving in the gods of the Athenian state and corrupting the youth of Athens. The prisoner Socrates, who was probably the greatest philosopher of the ancient world, believed both in God and immortality. When his judges suggested that the price of acquittal be the abandonment of his teaching, he replied, "I thank you, O Athenians, but I will obey God, who, as I believe, set me this task."  *83990*

The late afternoon sun filtering through the bars of his cell window reminded Socrates that when it set, he must die. Calmly and quietly he told his disciples of his faith that "to the good man no evil thing can happen in life or in death." Then just as the sun was sinking beneath the rim of the western horizon, Socrates drained the cup of poison hemlock handed him by the jailer, while his friends stood around him weeping. In a few moments he was dead. Plato, his most brilliant student, wrote this noble epitaph: "This was the end of our friend, a man, as we may say, the best of all of his time that we have known, and moreover the most wise and just." No sooner had Socrates died than the Athenians repented of this crime and some of his accusers, under public pressure, committed suicide. His name still commands admiration, honor, and high regard.

The story of Socrates' death is deeply moving, but the consequences of it on the world are vastly different from those that followed the death and resurrection of Jesus. Socrates died upholding the right to seek the truth. This high goal was doubtless also in the mind of Jesus, but Jesus gave his life to redeem mankind and to bring the human race in penitence and humility back to God. In his death men have seen the utter horror and brutality of sin but in his Cross and Resurrection they have seen the supreme manifestation of God's love to man. For as Paul says: "God was in Christ, reconciling the world unto himself." Socrates is still remembered with gratitude by the scholars of many nations, but to the rank and file of people he is only the echo of a name coming from a distant and almost forgotten period of history. Jesus Christ is revered and worshiped by hundreds of millions throughout the world as the revealer of God and the Saviour of men. The Resurrection has drawn the eyes of all men to Christ, the conqueror of death and the grave.

In a world like ours today, full of violence and the threat of death, the one person who has every right to remain undiscouraged and unafraid is the one who believes in eternal life. Personally, I should find it very difficult to face the future that awaits mankind were it not for the faith that whatever happens there still remains eternal life, that there are spiritual values that neither hydrogen bombs nor guided missiles can destroy. Jesus' revelation of eternal life robs death of its terror.

When the fear of death no longer holds sway over us, we have gained the most important victory that can come to anyone living in this vale of tears. Among the most significant words that Jesus ever uttered were these: "And I say unto you my friends, Be not afraid of them that kill the body, and after that have no more that they can do." Little wonder that the apostles of our Lord faced this last enemy of man with confidence and composure.

Eugene O'Neill pictures this truth dramatically in his remarkable play *Lazarus Laughed*. He tells how the brother of Martha and Mary, who had been raised from the dead by Jesus, had left the old home in Bethany and journeyed to Greece. In a square in Athens he meets the half-crazed and utterly cruel Gaius Caligula, who had been chosen by Tiberius Caesar as his successor. When Caligula was informed that the people hated him, he said, "Let them hate . . . so long as they fear us! We must keep death dangling before their eyes. . . . I like to watch men die."

Suddenly this wicked monster is confronted by Lazarus, who has the appearance of "a stranger from a far land." Caligula says to him, "So you're the man who teaches

people to laugh at death. . . . I fear everyone who lives."
Then he threatens Lazarus with execution. But Lazarus
looks into the face of Caligula, laughs softly "like a man
in love with God" and answers, "Death is dead, Caligula.
Death is dead." And the heir to the throne answers, "You
have murdered my only friend, Lazarus; Death would
have been [my friend] when I am Caesar." That is a true
representation of first century happenings. The resurrection of Jesus Christ made these early Christians fearless in
the face of death and completely unconquerable.

A Roman magistrate greets a Christian prisoner, standing in the dock before him, with these words, "I sentence
you to death for being a follower of the Nazarene." But
the prisoner looks unflinchingly into the eyes of the
magistrate and replies, "Sir, death is dead. It no longer
has power to make me afraid. Our divine Master has conquered death and the grave."

There is scarcely another text in the Bible that has
brought to me personally so much spiritual reassurance as
these words of our Lord: "Be not afraid of them that kill
the body, and after that have no more that they can do."

From the earliest years of my life I was taught by my
mother to believe that God would never abandon those
who put their trust in him. Well do I recall the closing
hours of her life. With the approach of death her faith
shone forth with unwonted splendor. I was just sixteen
years old at the time, yet I remember thinking that this
was her day of triumph, a triumph that crowned a life
lived in the service of Christ. She turned to me shortly
before the end and said, "Read to me the words from Isaiah
that tell of God's presence when we pass through the
waters." And I read:

But now thus saith the Lord that created thee, O Jacob, and he that formed thee, O Israel, Fear not: for I have redeemed thee, I have called thee by thy name; thou art mine. When thou passest through the waters, I will be with thee; and through the rivers, they shall not overflow thee. . . . For I am the Lord thy God, the Holy One of Israel, thy Saviour.

Years later, during World War I, when I found myself in situations on the battle front from which there seemed no hope of escape, these words came back to me with tremendous power. They breathed into my heart quietness and confidence.

Faith in the risen, living Christ enables us to meet confidently human situations that otherwise would leave us baffled and disheartened. Faith in eternal life makes it possible for us to believe the words of the poet: "The best is yet to be."

More Christians find solace and comfort in the words of the fourteenth chapter of John than in any other passage of the New Testament. On the black night of the betrayal our Lord said to his disciples:

Let not your heart be troubled: ye believe in God, believe also in me. In my Father's house are many mansions: if it were not so, I would have told you. I go to prepare a place for you. And if I go and prepare a place for you, I will come again, and receive you unto myself; that where I am, there ye may be also.

Here we have Christ's promise that at the end of our pilgrimage he will meet us and usher us into the Father's house on high. There we shall experience new disciplines, new opportunities for spiritual growth, and larger possibilities of service and worship in the heavenly Kingdom.

It was Charles Kingsley who remarked on one occasion: "God forgive me if it should be wrong, but I find myself looking forward to the life beyond with intense curiosity." Why should he have thought that this might be wrong? It is only natural that the thoughtful person will look forward eagerly to entering the new and untried experiences of a spiritual life where his dreams and hopes of the present may be fully realized.

So let us have done with pagan thoughts on life and death. Let us cast out of our Christian cemeteries the pagan symbols so often found there—the quenched torch, the broken column, the weeping willows. For these are symbols of defeat, frustration, and endless death. In their place let us exalt the Cross of the Resurrection, the empty Cross that is a symbol of victory over death and the grave. Above all, let us exalt the Christ who died and rose again, Lord of life, Conqueror of death, King of kings, Lord of lords, alive for evermore. As he lives, so shall we live also.

# NOTES

| Page | Line | |
|------|------|---|
| 10 | 26 | Job 14:11-12 |
| 13 | 28 | Charles E. Jefferson, *Things Fundamental,* used by permission of Thomas Y. Crowell Co. |
| 15 | 10 | John 17:3 (R.S.V.) |
| 16 | 17 | Jefferson, *op. cit.,* used by permission of Thomas Y. Crowell Co. |
| 18 | 5 | Bertrand Russell, *A Free Man's Worship* |
| 20 | 13 | Alfred Tennyson, "Ode on the Death of the Duke of Wellington" |
| 22 | 18 | I Cor. 13:12 |
| 22 | 21 | II Cor. 3:18 |
| 25 | 20 | "The Garden of Proserpine" |
| 26 | 30 | John 10:28 |
| 27 | 4 | John 10:10 |
| 27 | 16 | "The Two Voices" |
| 28 | 27 | John 14:2-3 (R.S.V.) |
| 29 | 4 | II Tim. 1:10 |
| 29 | 27 | Phil. 3:12 (R.S.V.) |
| 29 | 33 | "A Grammarian's Funeral" |
| 30 | 20 | Job 19:25 |
| 30 | 25 | Ps. 16:10-11 (R.S.V.) |
| 31 | 8 | Matt. 22:29-32 |
| 31 | 17 | Luke 20:38 |
| 31 | 21 | John 10:28 |
| 31 | 23 | Rom. 8:38-39 |
| 33 | 24 | John 10:29 |
| 34 | 31 | Luke 23:46 |
| 38 | 14 | "The Man Against the Sky," 1916, used by permission of The Macmillan Co. |
| 51 | 21 | John Greenleaf Whittier, "Yet Love Will Dream" |
| 52 | 4 | Ps. 30:5 |
| 53 | 3 | *The Search for Life's Meaning* |

95

| Page | Line | |
|---|---|---|
| 56 | 21 | Gen. 2:7 |
| 59 | 17 | II Cor. 5:4 |
| 60 | 5 | II Cor. 5:3 |
| 60 | 6 | I Cor. 15:38 |
| 60 | 7 | I Cor. 15:44 |
| 60 | 12 | I Cor. 15:50 |
| 61 | 1 | Heb. 12:1 |
| 62 | 1 | Heb. 12:1 |
| 62 | 13 | II Kings 6:17 |
| 62 | 25 | Acts 7:56 |
| 62 | 33 | Heb. 12:1 |
| 65 | 25 | *The Gospel of the Hereafter* |
| 67 | 13 | Luke 23:43 |
| 68 | 14 | Matt. 25:21 |
| 70 | 14 | "Retirement" |
| 71 | 8 | Rev. 22:3-4 |
| 71 | 21 | Matt. 25:21 |
| 73 | 8 | John 11:25-26 |
| 73 | 20 | John 11:25 |
| 73 | 23 | John 14:19 |
| 76 | 22 | Acts 4:5-10 |
| 77 | 24 | Acts 4:1-2 |
| 77 | 28 | Acts 4:33 |
| 78 | 7 | Acts 1:21-22 |
| 78 | 23 | Acts 2:22-24 |
| 79 | 8 | Gal. 1:13 (R.S.V.) |
| 79 | 11 | I Tim. 1:13 |
| 79 | 23 | II Tim. 2:8 |
| 79 | 32 | I Cor. 15:3-7 |
| 80 | 15 | Acts 5:41 |
| 81 | 8 | Used by permission of Oxford University Press, Inc. |
| 84 | 33 | II Cor. 5:17 |
| 85 | 1 | Gal. 2:20 |
| 85 | 2 | Phil. 4:13 |
| 85 | 33 | I Cor. 15:20-22 (R.S.V.) |
| 86 | 3 | I Cor. 6:14 |
| 87 | 4 | I Cor. 15:57 |
| 89 | 28 | II Cor. 5:19 |
| 90 | 16 | Luke 12:4 |
| 91 | 20 | Luke 12:4 |
| 92 | 1 | Isa. 43:1-3 |
| 92 | 21 | John 14:1-3 |

## Date Due

| | | |
|---|---|---|
| MAY 4 1959 | | |
| JAN 2 7 1960 | | |
| MR 8 '60 | | |
| MAY 2 3 1962 | | |
| MAY 1 1 '65 | | |
| MAY 2 5 '65 | | |
| JUN 3 '67 | | |
| OCT 1 0 1976 | | |
| | | |
| FEB 0 7 1970 | | |
| | | |
| | | |
| | | |
| | | |
| | | |
| | | |
| | | |
| ⒢Ⓑ | PRINTED | IN U. S. A. |